# Inspired
## to
# Succeed

Wit and Wisdom for
your Unlimted Success

# Dr. Stacia Pierce

1st Printing
Inspired to Suceed
ISBN: 978-0-9817734-0-7
Copyright © 2008  Dr. Stacia Pierce
Published by Life House Press
3000 W. Miller Rd.
Lansing, MI 48911

*Inspired to Succeed* is dedicated:

to my loving family, who provides me with inspiration
daily and makes success so worthwhile;

to my loyal staff for their commitment
and dedication to this project;

and to my partners and readers everywhere who desire
an exceptional life.  It's yours—be inspired to succeed!

# CONTENTS

# Inspired
## to
# Succeed

I am absolutely thrilled that you chose to pick up this book. Your decision to read *Inspired to Succeed* means you have just taken a monumental step in the direction of your dreams. As your life coach, I am here to show you how to achieve on a higher level. Consider every chapter in this book to be a one-on-one coaching session with me.

I have filled these pages with strategies and principles that have served me well on my journey to success. If you follow the keys and insights I share in each chapter, you will reach goals and find success that you may have never before thought possible. I penned this book with a heart to help you. Whatever your position or circumstance in life, you can break out of an average existence and live inspired! Each chapter is full of information and inspiration that is guaranteed to encourage, enlighten and empower you.

I want you to be encouraged to dream. This book contains heart-to-heart help that will cause you to live each day with high expectation and achievement. You will be enlightened on how to do, be and have better. These pages provide insight into exceptional living. Be empowered to rise higher. Leave mediocrity to the masses and gain a new sense of purpose and passion as you learn timeless principles of success that will cause you to excel in every area of your life.

You have a divine right to have the most prosperous and fulfilling life possible, but you must take purposeful steps to attain it. I am here to teach you how. All the information you need to be inspired to succeed is here in the palm of your hand. Like any good coach, I'm going to challenge you to stretch outside of your comfort zone and push you to take immediate action on what you read. But I will also be here cheering you on every step of the way because from this page forward, your life is never going to be the same again. Now, let's get going and begin what promises to be a dream-defining journey for you, as you get **inspired to succeed!**

## CHAPTER 1

# SMALL CHANGES, BIG RESULTS

**"Great acts are made up of small deeds."**
**-Lao Tzu**

Often when we think of changing our lives, we think of big projects and life-changing shifts—getting the body of a supermodel, buying our dream house or founding the next Fortune 500 company. We see the possibilities and often end up thinking big, *way too big*! We set ourselves up for failure by aspiring to do too much, too fast, all the while telling ourselves we failed because we didn't try hard enough. In actuality, the victory is not in trying harder, but starting smaller. Dream big, but execute small. A dramatic self-improvement campaign with a daunting deadline only increases your failure rate. When it comes to success in life, slow and steady usually wins the race.

> **Inch by inch,**
> **it's a cinch.**
> **Yard by yard,**
> **it's hard.**
> **-Unknown**

Ladies, it's time to adopt a new philosophy. Repeat after me, "I will make small changes for big results. I will get there little by little!" When you change your approach and focus on doing small things over the long haul, you'll realize huge gains toward your goals.

# Baby Steps

One of my favorite movies is *What About Bob?* In it, Bill Murray plays a patient named Bob, suffering from a hundred different worries and neuroses. To regain a normal life, Bob goes to see a psychiatrist for help. The psychiatrist encourages him to take baby steps to overcome his compulsions. His attempts to do this, although funny, eventually work. The storyline is made to be laughable, but the over-simplistic concept of baby steps rings true. You can benefit *greatly* from starting small!

# When to Think Small

**Go small if…**

- You're completely overwhelmed by your to-do list. ("I'm stretched too thin!")
- You feel paralyzed by the size of your goal. ("I could climb Mount Everest easier than achieving this.")
- You lack motivation to work toward your goal. ("I don't feel like it right now.")
- You find yourself procrastinating in multiple areas. ("I'll worry about that tomorrow.")
- You've lost hope that change is possible. ("I give up!")

The biggest benefit to making small changes is that it's more motivating and less time-consuming. Would you rather focus on going to the gym to walk a mile on the treadmill each day or practice parking a little farther from the front door each day? It's a small change, but it can have big results. We all know it's much easier to take small action steps than scale huge tasks, so adopt a new and smaller strategy. There's much truth to the childhood riddle: "How do you eat an elephant? One bite at a time." Simple, daily actions build momentum. Plus, the more small, daily victories you achieve, the more confidence you will feel, which will lead you to bigger and better things. The point is not to create a miracle moment, but to develop a better, more sustainable lifestyle. I experienced greater success in life when I learned to take a more balanced approach and make small adjustments that could be maintained over the long haul.

## The Tortoise and the Hare

In the race for the good life, we all can finish strong. I'm here as your life coach to cheer you on to the finish line and show you how to run well. Life is a marathon, not a sprint. That's where most people miss the secret to success. They underestimate the power of small steps. In looking for the monumental and trying to leap ahead, they overlook the power given to them to make life changes every single day. Greatness comes a little bit at a time. If they focused on copying my method rather than competing, they'd know that while they are looking for shortcuts, I just remain consistent at doing the little things that make a big difference. I might be taking small steps, but I never quit. Some days I'm more hare than tortoise and take steps faster than others, but every single day I am doing *something*. I'm moving one step closer to my dream.

Make changes that are congruent with your desires. Start heading in the right direction. You needn't get there overnight, just as long as you get there! There's something you *can* do daily. Too many times I hear women lament that it's so hard to change, but that's a cop-out. There's *something* small everyone can do to better their situation. A lot of small somethings eventually add up to a big something. And something small is always better than nothing at all. A little step toward success is still a step forward, not backward. Who I am today is who I've been all along. I developed myself through daily habits, year after year, and that's been the key to my success. I just stay steady and consistent and my lifestyle stays on the rise. Because this is how my husband and I live our lives, our children have learned to operate like this.

## A Penny a Day:  RYAN'S STORY

When my son was only five years old, I decided to start a fun project with him that would teach him the long-term value of saving money. I got a jar and encouraged him to save at least a penny a day. Whenever my husband and I would get change in the course of our day, we would add it to his collection. Coins seemed like such a small thing to us, but every little bit added up. At the end of every month, we would take him to the bank to see how much he had collected. On average, he would have a couple hundred dollars in just 30 days. As he grew older and my daughter saw how awesome this savings plan was working out for her brother, she decided to join in on the fun, but suggested we raise the ante to dollar bills. So, anytime we received single bills back from a purchase or found one in our billfold, we immediately took it out and set it aside for Ariana and Ryan. They too acquired the discipline of setting aside dollar bills. Sometimes they admitted it was tempting not to use the money out of convenience, but they stayed true to the small habit they had developed. We decided to wait until six months had passed before depositing the cash. As the stacks and stacks of dollar bills grew, it became so motivating for my children. When deposit day came, both of my children had more than $1,000 saved in single dollar bills. What started as a small change, yielded a big result. Now, more than six years later, my children have been doing this year after year, and they have saved a tremendous amount. Don't think this story is just an idea for your kids. Think like a child again yourself. It may feel like it's nothing when you're putting your two cents away, but it all adds up!

I recently shared this story with the women in my ministry and encouraged them to begin this habit in their lives. They eagerly stepped up to the challenge. Many of them took it one step further and signed up for a program a local bank was offering that rounded every purchase they made up to the nearest dollar and deposited the change in a savings account. Many ladies confessed this was the easiest change they ever made concerning their money and were loving the results! Small change, big result! What could you do with your money if you made a small change? What would happen if you passed up a coffee habit and instead saved the money you spend each day? What would be the long-term result of brown-bagging it for a period of time or slimming your shopping for a season? While I'm not telling you to give up on an abundant life and live like a simpleton, I am encouraging you to make some small changes now that will yield tremendous results later. It's worth it!

## Study Sessions:  ARIANA'S STORY

Since the time my daughter first started school, she's always been a self-disciplined student. Even as a young girl, she loved learning, and we encouraged her to make schoolwork a priority in her life. The older Ariana got, it seemed the more she excelled in school. We never had to tell her to do her homework or study for a test, because she practiced this every day without any prompting. It didn't matter whether we were on a plane headed on vacation or in the car running errands. Wherever we were, Ariana had her homework or a book in her lap, even if she would only have time for 15 minutes of study. Sometimes the trip seemed too short to warrant a bag of books, but Ariana was always one to seize even the smallest span of time to study more. Fast-forward to present day and Ariana's small steps have paid off grandly! She's a 4.0 student, the valedictorian of her class and can go to any university of her choice. What was once just 15 minutes of study saved thousands in tuition costs. Small change, big results!

Too often we get awed with the results of others and miss the process that got them there. Don't make the mistake of wanting to skip over the small stuff and become a big shot. When you cheat the system, you fail. It takes discipline and a lot of character to do the small stuff day in and day out. Master consistency without anxiety or hurry and you will want for nothing in days to come.

**Be faithful in small things, because it is in them that your strength lies.**
-Mother Teresa of Calcutta

## Small Changes You Can Make for Big Results!

■ **Write down your goals and read them every day.** I learned this habit from my husband. He has practiced this habit for more than 20 years. Every single morning, he writes down his goals again as if it's the first time. This hones his focus and often generates a host of ideas to help him achieve his objectives.

■ **Drink water.** Water is the best energy drink on the market. It has a host of benefits including eliminating toxins and poisons from your body, hydrating your skin, carrying nutrients and minerals and aiding weight loss. When your body is full of toxins, you don't think creatively. If you don't drink water, start with just one glass a day. Then slowly increase the quantity. Try adding one more glass each day until you reach 8-10 glasses a day.

■ **Exercise.** Exercise gives you more energy, powers up your day and boosts your self-esteem. Even if it's just 10 minutes a day, every little bit adds up. My daughter and I recently started running up and down our stairs for 10 minutes. After just a short session, our lungs feel expanded, our hearts are strengthened and our energy soars. Squeeze in walks during lunch hours or after an evening meal. Another way to fit in more exercise is to park farther from the door everywhere you go. Try adding just 50 more steps to your daily schedule. I invested in a pedometer so I can actually track my increased steps. I get most of my extra steps while power-shopping in the mall. Small change, big results!

■ **Clean every day for 10 minutes.** Sure, spring cleaning takes a lot longer, but you can create a sense of order and harmony in any room of your house just by tidying for 10 minutes each day. Add excellence to every room in your home. Clearing the clutter adds harmony, makes your home aesthetically pleasing and creates an environment conducive to creative thinking. The more welcoming your environment, the more you will produce there.

■ **Read 15 minutes a day.** So you can't read an entire book in one night. Just 15 minutes can give you a wealth of information that you wouldn't have had before. In fact, just 15 minutes of reading every single day over four year's time is equivalent to a bachelor's degree. Reading doesn't have to be lengthy to be beneficial. Even small bursts of positive information will change your outlook on life and cause you to be filled with information, strategies and ideas throughout your day. Reading truly is the key to succeeding.

■ **Work at work.** It doesn't take much to stand out from the office pack. Studies show that 87% of the work force won't work unless supervised. This means by simply working at work, you're in the top tier. Work hard and smart and you will be promoted often.  As employers, my husband and I know this to be true.  We always reward those who work well.  It doesn't take much.  Here are three basic skills that will always keep you employed:  Show up on time regularly.  Obey instructions.  Talk and act respectfully.  Master these and you'll always keep your job and your perspective.

## 30 More Small Things I Recommend:

1.  Hug your child or spouse.
2.  Write a daily To-Do list before you go to bed.
3.  Lay out your clothes the night before.
4.  Eat smaller portions.
5.  Listen more intently.
6.  Say "I love you" often.
7.  Do one thing you don't want to do each day.
8.  Buy books.
9.  Pray daily.
10. Read a chapter from the Bible daily.
11. Give big tips.
12. Say "thank you."
13. Compliment others.
14. Listen to positive audio messages.
15. Journalize often.
16. Eat breakfast every morning.
17. Find a reason to laugh daily.
18. Encourage your children.
19. Become your spouse's biggest cheerleader.
20. Travel more.
21. Buy quality over quantity.
22. Surround yourself with positive people.
23. Pay a little extra toward each bill, even if it's just cents.
24. Go to church a lot.

25. Eat healthy snacks.
26. Watch less TV.
27. Capture important memories with your camera.
28. Attend at least one conference a year.
29. Clear out the clutter.
30. Celebrate others' success.

No matter what your past excuse has been or the size of the goal you are up against, if you have the intention to change and make small, consistent steps over time, it works! Here's my challenge to you: test this out and see for yourself. For the next week, choose just one small thing to do differently and commit to it. At the end of the week, check out the results. If you like what you see, keep it up for a whole month. Soon you'll be on your way to a lifestyle habit and some big, big results!

SMALL CHANGES, BIG RESULTS
# Inspiration & Application:

■   **Dream big, but execute small.**

■   **Making small changes is more motivating and less time-consuming.**

■   **The point is not to create a miracle moment, but to develop a better, more sustainable lifestyle.**

■   **Make changes that are congruent with your desires. Start heading in the right direction.**

■   **There's something small everyone can do to better their situation.  A lot of small somethings eventually add up to a big something.**

## CHAPTER 2

# CELEBRATE LIFE ALWAYS

**"Celebrate the happiness that friends are always giving,
make every day a holiday and celebrate just living!"
-Amanda Bradley**

Life is a celebration. From the moment you were born, you were given the greatest gift you could ever receive—the gift of life! I believe the present is truly that—a present—a moment for you to enjoy the endless possibilities that lie on the road ahead. From the time I wake up, I celebrate life, just knowing today is another day for me to dream new dreams, pursue grand goals and improve myself if need be. You too can have a joyful journey just by choosing to make it so. Your life doesn't have to be boring. It can be as exciting as that of any supermodel or superhero. All you have to do is accept life's offer; it's asking you to jump in and join in the fun!

> I never lose sight
> of the fact that
> just being is fun.
> -Katharine Hepburn

Celebrating your life doesn't start when you slip a painted toe into your stilettos as you get glam for your next social event. Today needn't be your birthday for you to stop and celebrate. You can celebrate life every day. Each day, you get to be the guest of honor in your own life, so why not make it a party! Approach your job, mate, children and day with expectation and enthusiasm. Celebration is more than an event, it's an attitude—one that will greatly increase the quality of your lifestyle. So let's broaden our party perspective.

By my definition, women who celebrate life always are women who refuse to allow the mundane, an attitude of ungratefulness or a lack of appreciation to exist in their living space. In protest of the average, they live vibrantly, brightly and happily as if every day were a party. They appreciate every moment given to them and make the most of the life they have been blessed with. A life without celebration, gratitude and appreciation is lackluster. Don't choose to live that way.

> The more you praise and celebrate your life, the more there is in life to celebrate.
> -Oprah Winfrey

Instead, make a choice to enjoy life to the fullest. You've only been blessed with one life to live. So don't allow your life and the lives of those you love to pass by you unannounced. With all that God has provided us, it's a shame to live in day-to-day drab. In fact, I refuse to do it! I don't want to merely pass through life; I want to enjoy the journey. I love my full life and all the goals, commitments and to-do lists that come with it. It takes a daily focus and flexibility to keep up with the family, work, ministry and personal schedules we all juggle. Life would be dull without all these purposeful things to pursue. However, in striving to make a living, I make sure to have a life. Celebrations should be the exclamation points in a well-crafted life.

## The Art of the Party

I am a party planner by nature. Parties are my passion. I love them so much that I'm convinced a part of my call is to throw big bashes and grandiose galas. From planning the décor to running through the event schedule with my staff to choosing what goes in the goody bags, something about planning the hundreds of little details that go into these extravagant events brings out the best in me. Parties offer a burst of excitement for myself and my guests. Although it's a load of fun, it's far from frivolous. Party planning and entertaining is as important as your other daily work, so you must fit it in. People are valuable and worth celebrating.

Consider the following scenario. You are attending a theatre performance. At the end of an excellent scene, there is no reaction from the audience. Not one person claps, cheers or even smiles. Imagine if you were one of the performers. How would you feel? Under normal circumstances, most people would feel concerned or disappointed, if not completely devastated. It's easy to believe in and understand the importance of celebrating success in the theatre or sports arena, but so often we celebrate too little in the lives of those we love most. You may not be a party gal like me, but someone needs you to jumpstart the joy in their life. Someone needs you to say, "You're special" and love them lavishly with fanfare and festivities. Maybe it's your husband, your children, your girlfriends or your staff that needs a day to shine. In the end, we all need moments of celebration in our lives, and you can be the person who makes the difference.

Make time to celebrate. The reason I say "make" time is because planning parties does take time. When I throw events, I go to painstaking measures to ensure every detail will delight my guests. I plan every event to a "T" and add in the little surprising extras because that is the type of event I would want thrown for me. When guests attend these events, the comment I get the most is, "How did you find time to plan such an excellent event?" It's simple—I made the time. I realized a long time ago that there would never be a perfect day to plan a party. There is never a week when I can clear my entire schedule and plan the event from start to finish. However, I can make it fit *within* my schedule by purposing to do so. The party girl's motto is always: "Celebration and fun? It can be done!" Times of celebration are meant to be a lifestyle, not a luxury! It's necessary for an inspired life!

I take pleasure in bringing people together for a good time and wowing them with extravagant extras. I've thrown many a party, from posh, private affairs to guest lists that topped 500. Each has been a unique expression of my sense of style, my passion for people and my deep joy to celebrate others through giving. I could fill all the pages of this book delighting you with the details, but a picture is worth a thousand words, so you'll just have to get my DVD, *Inspiring Entertaining*. What I do want to share with you is the significance of celebration to truly living the good life. A timely celebration can forge friendships, kindle passion for purpose and enrich your family heritage. Take a pause for the cause as I take you inside three fabulous fétes. May they inspire you to remember and celebrate what and who is important in your life!

> **Life is too quick and too fabulous to let it slip by without raising a glass.**
> -David Tutera

## Welcome to Womanhood

I've always had a birthday party for my daughter, since the age of two. Every party has been full of meaning and has celebrated a chapter of her life. As the day for her 18th birthday neared, I knew I wanted to do something memorable for her big day that would pass down our family's values and celebrate this important rite of passage. I have always been inspired by the Jewish tradition of bat mitzvahs and Latina quinceaneras. I wanted to commemorate this very special year for my daughter by doing something substantial not only for her personally but for our Christian heritage. I wanted to start a new tradition in the body of Christ. This birthday was a celebration of her life and a graduation from being a young girl into a thriving woman, so I dubbed the theme "Welcome to Womanhood." I planned every detail of this party to be rich with meaning and significance. The night started with so much excitement. My daughter looked like a princess in her pink designer dress layered with tiers of pink tulle. To add to the pageantry, I orchestrated 17 of her closest friends to be her court. They looked resplendent, with the girls in gorgeous pink gowns and the guys in tuxedos. Hundreds of people were at the venue, with many of her closest friends from around the country flying in by private jet to celebrate her big day.

As the party began, each couple in the court strolled down the center aisle, bearing huge gift boxes. Each pair took their position on either side of an ornate golden throne centered on the stage, awaiting the guest of honor. Classical music played as the court waited with anticipation for the debutante's grand entrance. Next was a military salute, as officers from several branches of the armed forces marched in with precision and grace, drawing swords and creating a canopy for Ariana to walk under. When Ariana made her appearance, she looked every part of royalty. It was a moment I will never forget as she crossed over from a girl to a woman.

As Ariana took the stage and sat on her throne, my husband came and pronounced a blessing over her life. After the blessing came the meaningful goodies my husband and I had picked out to bless our daughter and signify her new "grown-woman" status. Each member of the court presented her with our gifts, including engraved, silver photo albums, engraved Chanel perfume, designer heels, a custom pink passport cover and a fabulous Louis Vuitton attaché for her laptop. These gifts were our way of preparing her to be a woman of culture and class. I would be remiss if I did not mention my husband later surprised Ariana by announcing that he was upgrading her H3 Hummer to the newest model! She almost fainted from excitement!

The evening continued as haute couture transitioned into hip-hop, infusing the evening with expressions of Ariana's personality and passions. The Life Changers Christian Center performing arts troupe showed incredible displays of drama, dance and step drill. The choir rocked the stage, bringing everyone to their feet as they remixed the popular song, "I'm Every Woman." The night came to a crescendo with video and vocal tributes from friends and mentors who wanted to welcome Ariana into womanhood with words of congratulations.

The entire affair was a rich tribute that has begun a tradition in the body of Christ. In the days that followed, I received tons of letters and emails from attendees, expressing how much the event meant to them and their children. The party was on the lips of all the teens at school for weeks and the parents of the kids on the court called to tell me how much it meant to their children to be a part of such a momentous occasion. The inquiries about the party spread to educators and youth ministries around the country wanting more details, so I decided to turn it into a DVD and make this tool available to all.

Whether you're a parent desiring to enrich your family's heritage or a group leader interested in replicating an event to welcome young people to adulthood in a significant way, it is my hope that this tool will help raise a new breed of young adults. Meaningful times of celebration in the lives of our children breed a higher level of success in them. That's why I never take my children's birthdays or special accomplishments lightly. You can use parties to promote your child's purpose, pass on family values and establish your family's code of conduct. It takes time and careful planning, but the results are worth it!

## My Bible Study Bashes

Being a part of my Bible study is like attending the largest girlfriend gathering every month. It's an atmosphere of grand celebration. Each month I choose a different theme that I bring to life in a fashionably elegant way. Just walking in the room is electrifying. I've seen women cry at the door from being so overwhelmed, not only by the beauty and grandeur, but also by the love and kindness that fills the room and emanates from my ladies. One woman, who traveled hours to attend, said she had heard of the incredible things that were happening at Successful Living Bible Study, but thought a Bible study like this could only be a fantasy. After she came and experienced it for herself, she said it really was a dream come true for her. Why do I go to such great lengths to make an impression? Because I believe that being a Christian should be fun. I am inspired to live my life in a big way and help others to do the same. Ladies, life is huge!

I have put on such spectacular events that now the women themselves want to come to my events in a spectacular way. One out-of-town group that attends the Bible study decided to rent stretch Hummer limousines and bring their entire group of 75 ladies to Bible study in style. It was an awesome sight to see and it set their expectations for the night on a high level. Many of them had never ridden in a limousine before, but because of my Bible study event they began to dream on the next level and experience on the next level. I've been told that the word is out. Ladies know that if they are in one of my areas, my Bible study is the place to be. They enjoy the empowering, girly time just for them.

Every woman deserves time designated solely to her personal growth and nurturing. Women give so much. That's why they love Successful Living Bible Study because it's all about giving to them. Ladies from the East Coast to the Midwest don't think twice about coming because they tell me it's a night they need. I even created a private Bible study for my celebrity friends so they can be inspired and encouraged in an atmosphere that is conducive to them. No matter which of the Bible studies ladies attend, they love it because it's a celebration in their honor they never forget. Attending celebrations like these help transform a life of predictable pursuits into a legacy of merriment and meaning.

## A Stylish Staff Soiree

This party was my way of celebrating my staff and letting them know I was concerned about their work, but also their look. At this party, I challenged each of my guests to create a storyboard of their ideal work wardrobe. I had tables and tables filled with the latest issues of every fashion magazine on the market. With lively music playing in the background, the fun began. While my guests and I busied ourselves cutting and pasting fashionable looks on our boards, the shop talk began. I shared with them all the "It Items" for spring and educated them on the look that would work best for each of them. Everyone got a chance to showcase her board and show off her new look. Then the party moved to my closet, where I gave the girls a peek at my latest purchases of shoes, jewelry, clothes and coats, leaving them bubbly with excitement. When the night was done, each girl left with fashionable goodies I gave them as parting gifts and their faith prop for their new look. Within weeks, I noticed improvements in their image. Instead of a relaxed day job look, their image said "high-power executive." The party accomplished its goal, but in a fun and innovative way. That was my creative way of doing a performance review. All work and no play can make you dull and drab, so keep your life and look poppin'! These are just three of many celebrations that I have hosted to add fun and flair to my life and others. Don't wait for an occasion to celebrate. Whether you are the guest of honor or the host with the most, celebrate life every day and in every way. Life is a continual party when you purpose for it to be. Consider this your exclusive invitation to join in on the fun!

CELEBRATE LIFE ALWAYS

# Inspiration & Application:

- The present is truly that—a present—a moment for you to enjoy the endless possibilities that lie on the road ahead.

- Celebration is more than an event, it's an attitude—one that will greatly increase the quality of your lifestyle.

- Don't allow your life and the lives of those you love to pass you by unannounced.

- Celebration is a vital part of the good life. Learn to celebrate every day in every way.

- You can use parties to promote your child's purpose, pass on family values and establish your family's code of conduct.

## CHAPTER 3

# LIVE GORGEOUSLY

**"Zest is the secret of all beauty.
There is no beauty that is attractive without zest."
-Christian Dior**

I wholeheartedly concur, Monsieur Dior! Being gorgeous is not for the weak. It takes strength, discipline and dare I say zeal to refuse the acceptable, preferring instead the exceptional. Do you want to be adequate or astonishing? You are perfectly within your rights to be exceptional, extraordinary and divine. Some may consider this an elitist attitude, but isn't that why we are here—to be the best we can be? Why live, if you are not living? Support on your road to gorgeous living will be sparse. I, however, will always be on the sidelines cheering as you endeavor to pursue the best. Today is the day to acquire an appetite for being amazing.

**We ask ourselves, who am I to be brilliant, gorgeous, talented, and fabulous? Actually, who are you not to be? You are a child of God.**
-Marianne Williamson

Living gorgeously is about being the entire package, not just a one-trick pony. You should be beautiful *and* smart. Living gorgeously is allowing your inner substance to reveal itself in a substantially attractive expression. Brains and beauty are not required to be mutually exclusive of one another. In my book, *The Good Life Guide to Beauty*, I dedicated a chapter to bashing your beauty bully. A beauty bully is that little voice telling you the effort required to be impeccable is frivolous and unnecessary. I am here to tell you that your effort, or lack thereof, can and will make a difference in your life. You will only receive the opportunities in life that you are prepared for. Your appearance is the key that opens the door and gives your highly advanced intellect an opportunity to shine.

I am a glamour girl and I never apologize for that. I am a modern, contemporary woman who knows a truly feminine woman carries a powerful presence. I relish all things feminine, from lipsticks and lotions to handbags and haute couture—if it's girly, I've got it—in spades. I can mix it up in the boardroom and the beauty salon. You will never mistake me for simple Cymbeline, for whom playwright William Shakespeare noted: "her beauty and her brain go not together." I'm talking about style and substance, sister! The road to gorgeous living begins right here. Now is the time to get it tight and right. Begin building a blueprint for your own unique and extraordinary beauty.

## Gorgeous Girls are Adamant About Upkeep

Living gorgeously often means that what others consider indulgent should be your necessities. We live in a fast-paced world, but gorgeous girls never lag behind in the upkeep department. Learn to take the time to get *really* ready. Stop walking out the door without giving yourself a thorough once-over. Do you really look your best today? What reason could there be for not putting your best face forward? Whatever reason you *think* you have: the kids, the alarm or the all-night project, I'm here to tell you that it is no a good enough excuse for personal neglect.

Package yourself for success. Everyone is a salesperson in this world and if you can't buy into your own beauty, you can't expect others to buy into your success. Don't get lazy or lax with your looks. Make a commitment today to really take care of yourself each and every day.

> **There is no such thing as an ugly woman, only a lazy one.**
> -Helena Rubinstein

I know a lady who has a 45-minute commute to work and is required to be at her desk by 7:30 am. She gets herself up, washes, blow dries and properly curls her hair, gets dressed, wakes up her two daughters, dresses them immaculately with matching hair accessories and is never late. She arrives to work fully made up every day. Her coworkers chastised her for years, telling her it was perfectly OK if she missed a step in the process; no one really saw them anyway since most of their work was via telephone. Why bother? She never answered her critics; she just continued her daily routine, day after day, year after year. That's a woman who is living gorgeously. There may not be an external reason for what she did, but internally she had a conviction that she and her daughters were important enough to look their very best every day. She gets my vote for gorgeous girl. This exhibits what we already know: Critics always know the cost of everything, but neglect acknowledging the true value. The cost of being gorgeous is paid in discipline, forethought and effort, but the value of high self-esteem and fearless confidence is invaluable.

Speaking of cost, always remember, money does not make you gorgeous. Today, I have the privilege of buying top-of-the-line clothes, makeup and accessories, but what really makes me walk confidently are the fundamentals I mastered before I could afford the designer goods. Here are a few pointers from my primer for creating a polished appearance: Never underestimate the power of clean. Soap and water can be attained for a bargain, but they reap a cache of wealth in self-esteem and self-respect. Develop a bathing ritual that cultivates self-care. Become skilled at caring for your body. Do not allow another sunset to lapse without immersing yourself fully in water. I lean into luxury with scented shower gels during my long and luxurious showers and pamper myself with lotions, perfumes and powders afterward. When I have even more time, I surround my bathtub with scented candles, turn on the stereo and wash the cares of the world away. Sure, you may be accustomed to a quick shower, but set the bar higher than the status quo. Once you really embrace the ritual of bathing and not just washing, you will improve the way you admire and appreciate yourself.

## Gorgeous Girls Look Good Around the Clock

Living gorgeously means considering all the details of your life. Are you just pulling it together when all eyes are on you? I decided years ago that I would be gorgeous all the time, even when no one was looking. I invested in beautiful pajamas and daywear for those times when I am lounging around the house. I even have my pajamas tailored so they fit perfectly. If you can have house shoes, why not house clothes? It's another reason to shop, ladies! Self-check time: If someone rings your bell at night, what are they likely to encounter? Oversized T-shirts from college and cartoon-themed, oversized slippers? Perhaps Grandma's old house dress, passed down to a new generation? Come on girl, get gorgeous *for real*. It's what people don't see that reveals the most about you.

Invest in your quiet time. Buy cotton, silk or terry cloth sets that caress you after a hard day's work. I have so many great options for my home life. Some are classic pajamas, others are cut like track suits with a pant, a tank and a zip-up jacket for discretion. There is a whole world of loungewear available to enjoy on any budget.  Make a plan to buy a set this weekend and see the difference it makes in how you feel.  I promise you will sleep better and wake up happier.  That is gorgeous living!

## Gorgeous Girls Put Forth Effort

Become passionately zealous about yourself again.  An image that appears effortless takes a lot of energy, no matter what those glossy magazines would have you believe.  Natural beauty is rare; we all need enhancing and maintenance.  Learn the importance of impeccable maintenance because that is the little-known key to image and health preservation.

There's an ancient French proverb that says, "A woman is no older than she looks." Europeans are known for aging well and they attribute it to their personal care regimens.   From their youth, girls are drilled to take proper care of their skin. C'est magnifique!  Take a tip from these fabulous femmes; you will look better and younger longer when you put in more authentic maintenance time. If you speak with your hands, what are they saying?  Hopefully, they are not screaming for a hydrating manicure.  If you are walking into a bright future, are your feet properly pedicured for the trip?  Have you been maintaining your million-dollar smile?  Are your teeth clean, bright and gorgeous?  Do your clothes look effortlessly chic or just effortless? my Image Course, clothing care, such as washing and ironing, is stressed. We actually have someone demonstrate how to properly iron a shirt, a pair of pants and a skirt.  Crisp, clean clothes make the man—and the

> A beautiful woman doesn't have to choose between living a great life and looking ten years younger. Living a great life can lead to looking ten years younger. Now, that's beautiful.
> -Laurie Pawlik-Kienlen

man—and the woman.   That clean, fresh, "I take care of myself" look will always give you the edge in any social situation.  To look unforced and naturally chic surely requires effort, but the payoff is walking out the door ready to diligently pursue your plans and dreams without the restraint of insecurity.

## Gorgeous Girls Set New Standards

Have high style.  Living gorgeously requires you to raise your standards.  Living above the norm will require you to know more, ask for more and sometimes even insist for better.  I always say, "people do what you inspect, not what you expect." Scrutinize everything about your beauty regimen.  You don't just have to settle for a good haircut, you must have a gorgeous one. Go to your stylist with a vision in hand for your hair or makeup look.  Work directly with your technician and demand that they give you the best possible interpretation of that look.  Don't accept their cookie-cutter daily special—this is your image we are talking about here!  I am very particular about my manicures and pedicures.

**Gorgeous hair is the best revenge.**
-Ivana Trump

I let my manicurist know exactly what I want and I compensate her for giving me exceptional service. Most professional technicians want your creative input and your positive feedback.  It helps them sharpen their technique when they know you expect and appreciate their absolute best.  If your usual technician is offended by your courteous collaboration, it's time to find someone else.  Only the best technicians can give you the expertise that will result in your best look.

Never adjust to average.  Have a special air about you.  Add a "WOW" factor to your life.  What makes your life go wow?  What makes your marriage go wow?  What makes your image go wow?

Glamour! Add glamour wherever you can. Make the effort in every area of your life to do more than just exist. Put more effort into making your life and yourself better. Accessorize your look and your life. Accessories always add glamour. Don't just wear pants and a top; add a stunning bag or outstanding shoes to make your outfit pop! Don't just waste the weekend; throw a lavish dinner party with a few of your closest friends. Buy some new music and have a sampling party. Take your children to the theatre. Accessorize your life with good times, meaningful relationships and beautiful things. An accessorized life is a gorgeous one.

Begin to collect pieces that totally excite you. Whenever I am shopping for anything, whether it's makeup, clothes, shoes or furniture, my selections must totally excite me for me to make a purchase. I do not wish to tolerate the boring or hum drum in my personal space. My glamour and wow factors stay at high levels due to my attention to details and my enthusiasm about personal upkeep and maintaining an inspiring living space. Get excited about who you are and the life you've been blessed with. Don't let your life stay in the rut of the regular.

All of these tips are a part of my glamour equation. Do the math for yourself: your image plus your confidence equals the doors that will open for you in life. The level of care you give yourself is in direct proportion to the level of respect others will give you. If you want others to care, then you should care more. You will only have the gorgeous life you are willing to create for yourself. If you take these action steps and increase your care quota, I can guarantee your success quotient will take you to new and inspiring places.

LIVE GORGEOUSLY

# Inspiration & Application:

- The cost of being gorgeous is paid in discipline, forethought and effort, but the value of high self-esteem and fearless confidence is invaluable.

- Living gorgeously means considering all the details of your life.

- Become passionately zealous about yourself again.

- Living above the norm will require you to know more, ask for more and sometimes even insist for better.

- Accessorize your life with good times, meaningful relationships and beautiful things. An accessorized life is a gorgeous one.

---

CHAPTER 4

---

# PURPOSEFULLY PLAN

**"It takes as much energy to wish as it does to plan."**
**-Eleanor Roosevelt**

Planning is a lifestyle. But I promise not to bore you to sleep with a drawn-out speech on goal-setting and time management. And I certainly won't pull out charts and graphs and try to color-code your schedule for you. Instead, I want to charge you to get creative and challenge yourself to change. Being a planner isn't hard; it's easy, creative and fun. It's what you do to make all the people, passions and projects in your world fit. Being a master planner is about learning how you can fulfill your potential while still balancing your life. Girls, no matter what you're a guru at—be it raising children or raising capital—this chapter is for you! Today's woman has her hands in many things—raising a successful family, volunteering in the church, running a business or running for office.

The world is ripe with opportunities and possibilities for any woman who is a planner. Although I have always purposed to live life well, I would never have dreamed how far the principles of planning could have taken me. Today, my purpose involves different components—writing books, ministering around the country, co-pastoring Life Changers Christian Center alongside my husband, raising a family, managing a staff and running a business. I wouldn't be able to do all the things I do if I didn't learn how to master my time by having a plan. I am where I am because I plan where and what I want to be. I am a master planner. I have been operating like this for years. I plan everything, and I really mean everything. I plan what I will wear daily, what foods we will eat in our home, our vacations, my itinerary, etc. If there is to be a successful purpose for anything, it will require a plan.

I've learned during the years that the better I plan, the better I become at doing more than one thing. I can be a mother, a bestselling author, an executive, an entrepreneur, a motivational speaker, a wife and a mentor and I still have time to enjoy life. My plan increases my productivity, and my productivity increases my profitability. I am busier than I have ever been, but I produce more. Planning is the hidden secret behind my successful life.

Girls, I want you to grasp the power of planning. Life is as worthwhile as you plan for it to be. There are just some things that you will never be able to accomplish until you become a more purposeful planner. You can have the talent, the money and even the position, but if you lack a plan for your day and your life, you won't achieve like you should. Having a plan helps you put into place the organization necessary to meet your goals.

## Louis and Me

Louis Vuitton is one of my favorite stores. I love the handbags, shoes and life accessories. Rarely do I travel without making a stop in a LV store. It stands to reason that one of my most important tools comes from the Vuitton lineage. I carry a multicolor monogram agenda created for Louis Vuitton by designer Takashi Murakami. A gift from one of my dearest friends and essential to my daily planning, I never leave home without it. Inside it are my written plans detailing everything I need at a glance. Not only does it contain my goals for the year and my to-do lists, but it also stores my shopping list of the clothes I want for the upcoming season, a list of all my speaking engagements, a list of gifts I need to purchase for upcoming occasions, my confessions, my family vacation schedule and a few messages in case I have to minister somewhere unexpectedly. This doesn't prevent interruptions, but it helps me to keep flowing no matter what arises. I'm not extreme where I plan every minute; I just know that a day that's not planned is often stolen and wasted away. Life is much too precious for that. I plan to spend time with my husband, I plan to play with my kids and I plan to complete my God-given assignments. I plan my travel itinerary, Bible study events, conferences, church events and vacations all at least a year ahead of time. My secretary, personal assistant, nannies, household staff and I all sit down once a week to review and coordinate schedules so everything at home and work runs smoothly. When it comes to being effective at multi-tasking, you must have a plan. Life doesn't get good until you get a plan. A successful life is an intentional life. Develop a plan for everything.

## Ten Plans You Should Have in Place

1. Plan your wardrobe. Create a list of items you need to upgrade your look for the upcoming season. Assign outfits you will wear to specific events. Plan when and where you will take shopping trips and how much you will spend.

2. Plan your vacations. Determine where and when you want to go. Create a budget for your trip and make detailed preparation plans.

3. Plan your finances. Plan how much you want to sow, save and

spend. Plan how much money you want to earn this year and get creative about strategizing new streams of income.

4. Plan your marriage. Set aside time in your schedule for romantic outings and vision sharing. Plan to be intimate often.

5. Plan your meals. Write down your menu for the week or even the month. Plan when you will grocery shop and create a grocery budget. Plan healthy snacks for you and your family.

6. Plan your personal growth. Set aside funds for books, seminars and courses. Write down a reading plan and create a list of books to purchase. Set personal growth goals and execute your plan.

7. Plan your spiritual walk. Make a plan for your prayer time and Bible study. Plan to be at church a lot and to make church a priority in your family's life. To make attending service easier, plan what you and your family will be wearing the night before.

8. Plan your relationships. Plan outings with your girlfriends and gifts you want to give.

9. Plan your children's development. Plan out the activities, camps and programs you want your children to be involved in. Plan personal growth outings and adventures to take with them. Plan special time together as a family and alone time with each child so you can pour into them. This affirms their self-esteem and helps them grow.

10. Plan your life's end. I don't mean to be morbid or morose, but it's good to have plans in place for when you pass so it doesn't fall

on your children. Plan where and how you want to be buried and make sure you have enough life insurance to leave an inheritance and cover funeral expenses.

# Family Planning

I plan to have a good marriage by scheduling date nights once a week with my husband. I schedule "dream days" where my husband and I freely share our hearts, hopes and dreams. You have to plan this kind of communication. You must purpose to be intimate. Plan your romance. I love spontaneous gifts and unexpected gestures of love from my husband, but those are just icing on the cake. My husband and I have a successful marriage because we plan on purpose every year to take our marriage up a level.

I also plan for our family to be successful. I plan good family vacations every year with my children. We sit down at the start of each year and discuss where everyone wants to travel. Then we plan the trip itinerary and create a financial plan so we have the resources we need to fully enjoy ourselves on the trip. Good vacations are a result of having a plan.

We also plan our goals as a family. In our annual goal-setting meetings, we include our personal assistants, our domestic care manager and our child care assistant, because their role is important in keeping our home running smoothly. During this meeting, everyone shares their goals for the year and their plan for achieving their goals. We talk about ways we can support one another in reaching our goals and pray over them. Then, we execute our plan throughout the year. Because we have raised our children from a very young age to be planners, they achieve big too. Whatever you are, you pass down. Girls, it's time to pass down a legacy of achievement by teaching your children to plan! If you want life to get better, plan better—for everything. The plan you execute every day determines the direction of your life. Learn to plan well. Let me share with you my fail-proof planning process. It works!

## 1. Plan Your Day

Begin by sitting down and planning tomorrow. Get a plain piece of paper and pen. Decide on a time to wake up—write that down. What will you wear tomorrow? What will your children wear? Write that down. What will you eat for breakfast? Write that down. Will you take your lunch, or will you eat out? Write a plan for your workday, hour by hour. When will you review and respond to email? What phone calls need to be made, correspondence typed? Write that down too. What are you having for dinner? What family, social or personal activities will you do following dinner? Write it all down now. Now stop and take a look: you have just produced a plan for the day. If this is your first daily plan, give yourself a high-five, you deserve it.

Now that you have accomplished the 'what' of your day, you need to execute the 'how'. Get up from where you are sitting now and allow your plan to produce purposeful action. Set your alarm. Grab your clothes and prepare them. If lunch needs to be packed, get it ready. Set the breakfast table now. Put your files in your bag and set the bag by the door. Wake up to an alarm with a purpose for your day and notice how your joy level and productivity increase. No plan is perfect; there will always be modifications along the way, but the point is that now you actually have a way, instead of the day having its way with you.

## 2. Plan with Pictures

Planning on paper is a major key to successful execution, but learning to use visualization effectively will exponentially increase your execution level. There is a visual component to every project I am working on. There is nothing I have accomplished that I did not see first. I have used the process of visualization with great success for years. I invented my best-selling dream tool, the Prayer & Purpose Planner, based on this practice. People were always astonished at my high level of accomplishment and I became inspired to produce a tool that would help them plan and visualize their success. After many years, the method has proven itself, with stacks of testimonials of success from everyone who uses it. Letters still pour in to this day from people who have gained dream homes, jobs, cars and even true love. When you conceive it, you can achieve it!

I Prayer & Purpose Plan *everything*! Inside my Prayer & Purpose Planner, I can visually see every facet of my life and future. I begin picture planning by gathering my inspiration with scissors in hand. I find photos from magazines that correspond to what I want to achieve or acquire. Gather what intrigues you. This process of hunting and gathering is the method that helps you to live an inspiring life. With my clippings in hand, I paste words and phrases on a Planner Page to help stimulate me and give more clarity to my vision. Once my collage is complete, I put it in full view. Ideas and strategies come to me on how I can make what I see on the page come to life. The process works. Whatever you see each day, you will begin to work toward. Do you have an inspiring visual plan to focus on? If not, create one today. View my Planner pages and read others' Planner success stories on my website, **www.ministry4women.com**.

Visualize new things so you can plan better. My hairdresser has a 7-

foot-tall storyboard of all the latest hairstyles for the season, so when clients come in to get their hair done they can easily plan a new look using the pictures on the board. It's a simple and inexpensive prop, but it generates a lot of referral business because clients know she stays current on hair trends and can visually direct them to a style that will look great. Purposefully plan according to what you are called to do. A picture is *still* worth a thousand words!

## 3. Work Your Plan

Once you've set your plan, you must get busy executing your plan. I begin each day with the attitude that I will do whatever is necessary to get whatever I need to complete for the day done. Sometimes

> **Those who are victorious plan effectively and change decisively.**
> -Sun Tzu

this may mean staying up extra hours or tackling the hardest thing first. The work I put into planning my life is in vain if I'm not willing to work to execute the plan. Focus on making progress daily at putting your plans into action. Even when diversions come, deal with them and get right back on track. Don't lose your focus when circumstances change, just get flexible. Revisit your plan and tweak whatever is not working. Sometimes you may be unsure how you are going to achieve your plan, but say aloud "I can do it!" anyway. Your words have creative power. If you let God direct you, He'll always show up with a strategy. Stick to your daily plan and carry it out to the best of your ability, no matter what!

Being a master planner takes work, but the work ends with a profit. Increase is on the other side of increased productivity and planning. You can put your life on a new track by learning that hard planning paves the way to hard cash. You are power-packed for accomplishment. Roll up your sleeves, darling, it's time to go to work. You can live stress-free and well-planned even if you're habitually unorganized and prone to spontaneity. Just change your attitude and get started today. Do something. Plan your house cleaning routine. Write a to-do list for tomorrow. Make a family schedule. Just do something now and get the good times rolling!

PURPOSEFULLY PLAN

# Inspiration & Application:

- **Life is as worthwhile as you plan for it to be. If you want life to get better, plan better—for everything.**

- **Planning is a lifestyle, not a task. A successful life is an intentional life.**

- **Wake up to an alarm with a purpose for your day and notice how your joy level and productivity increase.**

- **Planning on paper is a major key to successful execution, but learning to use visualization effectively will exponentially increase your execution level.**

- **The plan you execute every day determines the direction of your life.**

## CHAPTER 5

# CREATE A FASHIONABLE LIFE

*"Fashion is not something that exists in dresses only.*
*Fashion is in the sky, in the street, fashion has to do with ideas,*
*the way we live, what is happening."*
-Coco Chanel

Mademoiselle Chanel was a leading pioneer in fashionable living She was one of the first designers to realize the business of fashion and how it represented life in motion. Today, her apartment in Paris is exactly the way she left it and her fashion philosophy is all over it. From the color scheme to the famous Coromandel screens that relayed her love of the Orient, to her iconic initials printed on her table service. Her legacy of style lingers today, with each fashion season reinterpreting the well-known Chanel look. Only a woman can grasp this trend, because generally women are emotionally in touch with their surroundings, intent in their endeavor to make everything more beautiful, more inviting and personally inspiring.

Fashion does not end when you close your closet door. You are your fingerprint and how you live shows what mark you have decided to leave behind. Life can be dull, unexciting and unspectacular or it can be inspiring, over the top and magnificent— all by how you choose to style it. Your life, personal space and everything you inhabit is a visual display of what you think, dream and believe. Fashionable living is that expression.

# Fashion Defined

Fashion means "manner" or "style", but it's more than just clothes. A fashionable life is a life well above average. It's an existence watermarked with your values, personal style and quality standards. It's allowing the essence of who you are to permeate your environment. I've adopted fashionable living as my lifestyle and now my life takes on greater meaning and importance. The thread count on my sheets is significant, the color of my toothbrush counts and it makes a difference that my clothes are arranged neatly in my closet, in color-coded order with matching hangers. It does carry some weight that my luggage is color-coordinated. It all matters, because it all represents me—and I matter. My family is important, and my life is important. There is no one else like you on this earth; shouldn't you think that is relevant and worthy of expression?

I decided years ago that I would leave my fingerprint on this time as a testimony that life can be an exhilarating adventure. Why work to pay others and not pay myself back with what I like and enjoy? As a street-wise disco queen once said, "She works hard for the money" I say, learn to treat yourself right. I made it my mission to upgrade, update and invigorate my environment in any way possible. You too should look over the landscape of your life and grade it. Are you flunking in style and needing a refresher course in beautiful living?

> Have nothing in your home that you do not know to be useful and believe to be beautiful.
> -William Morris

Stop and do a test right now. Put the book down; I will be here when you get back.

Walk outside your home with a piece of paper and pen, closing the door behind you. Take a deep breath and walk back in, but this time, look at your environment as if you had never seen it before.

Look at it as if it was a total stranger's house and you had to give a three-word description of the people who lived there based on what you saw. What three words would they be? Be brutally honest. If you like the three words you chose, keep reading. You'll be motivated and inspired to make even more life improvements. If you don't like the three words, keep reading, this chapter will change your life forever.

## Fashion is Fresh

Get clean and organized. Fashionable living is not filthy. Develop a proper and thorough system for cleaning your home. Go to a dollar store and buy a bucket for each room. Buy a bunch of spray bottles. Then buy a large container of the proper cleaners for each aspect of the room—the glass, the wood, the counters, etc. If money is an object, then buy one to two bottles of each cleaner and split the solution among the empty spray bottles. Get a roll of paper towel, rubber gloves (don't mess up your manicure) and sponge for each bucket. Put each bucket in a cabinet in every room. Now, you have a proper cleaning bucket for each room. One of the hindrances of keeping an area clean is the trek to another room or the linen closet to get the proper products. Now that you have your bucket, you can quickly do a wipe-down of each room after use.

Make it a household responsibility for everyone in your family, explaining that in order to enjoy a fresh and clean home, it will require everyone pitching in their share of elbow grease. Good luck with that announcement; I know it may take some more time than others to realize the benefits and do their share. Even if they don't, keeping the house clean and neat should still be a priority for someone. I must emphasize that if no one else in your home wants to get on your new bandwagon of clean living, put on your rubber gloves, grab your bucket and keep scrubbing.

## Fashion is Functional

Make it a priority to maintain what matters and—what have we already established?—it all matters. Start taking better care of what you have now—if something is broken, fix it right away. Don't fool us into thinking you are living gorgeously and upon our visit, we discover you abide in a broke-down palace. Every woman should have a basic tool kit and a general working knowledge of how to use the tools. Most big chain stores have a compact tool kit for ladies (it often comes in pink!) that you can get for less than $20. It contains a pair of pliers, a wrench, two basic screwdrivers, a hammer and pack of nails, scissors and a tape measure. This should get you through most basic household non-emergencies.

Being helpless is not attractive, so learn how to do a few things yourself. You should be able to retighten a loose screw and hammer a nail into the wall to hang a picture if needed. Now that you have your tool kit, become handy around the house. Put that knob back on the cabinet. Go to the store and replace the phone cord that keeps providing embarrassing pauses in your conversations. Finally, hang that art on the wall. If in doubt—find out. With Internet access, you can simply type in, "How should I hang a mirror?" and tons of do-it-yourself guides will appear. Forget the Honey-do list or waiting for your brother to "stop by" and do it yourself. Declare this Friday night "fix it night": put on your pink tool belt and join the home care revolution.

**Nothing is in good taste unless it suits the way you live. What's practical is beautiful... and suitability always overrules fashion.**
-Billy Baldwin

## Fashion is Fully Stocked

We are almost to the fun part, but the next to-do of fashionable living is to stock what makes your house run efficiently. You can never be inspired to think next-level thoughts when your existence is full of small daily frustrations. If your home runs like a Swiss watch, it will free you to pursue and achieve more. Build a pantry of essential items that you will always need, but are a nuisance when you run out. We all know what falls under this category— batteries, garbage bags, light bulbs, dish detergent, dishwashing soap, laundry powder, etc. There is nothing more frustrating than realizing you just used the last square of tissue.

It is never convenient to run to the store for these items—when you need them, you really need them. I made it a practice to buy these items in bulk. Of course, you may need to build up to that. Start with buying two packs of light bulbs. Then next time, buy one more; eventually you will accumulate a stash. Limit the irritation in your life by preparing your home to run proficiently. Fashionable living is learning to run on optimum efficiency, because it is never fashionable to be frazzled.

Now that you have cleaned, organized, repaired and become efficient, you are on level playing ground. The first part was necessary because most people want to skip to the fabric, paint and pillows without laying the foundation of living well. Who cares if your home is decorated well, if it smells dirty? That's like putting a dress on a pig and no one would do that, right? But now that all of that is behind us and we are working with the proverbial clean slate, let us find our box of crayons and begin coloring your world. The late vaudevillian actor Danny Kaye, who was known for his colorful personality, once said, "Life is a great big canvas, and you should throw all the paint on it you can." I agree!

## Fashion is Custom-Fitted

Inspire yourself. Bring your fashion sense home with you. Incorporate it into your car, china, clothes, décor and personal pursuits. Surround yourself with your own brand of chic and style. You are a designer original, so your lifestyle should nourish and feed you to accomplish your dreams.

This year I decided to use my style sense to upgrade my personal spaces. While flipping through the digital pictures on my camera one day, I was struck by how many incredible moments I had captured. I had lifestyle photos of my family at grand events, photos of us hanging out with celebrities in our circle, and candid shots of us laughing and playing in various settings. I wanted to display these in an impactful way and bring our world to life. I walked through my home and the idea struck me to create a photo foyer. In my mind's eye, I saw a picture wall featuring a grand display of family photos from floor to ceiling. I did a bit of research and found some beautiful, custom frames that overlaid each other in an intricate pattern, much like a Chinese jigsaw. Once the photos were printed and placed in the frames, the wall montage was breathtaking.

My foyer went from flat to fashionable! Now, everyone who walks in my home gets an insider's view of our lifestyle and a dose of how much fun we have together. I can hardly tear away company from the wall as they stand enamored and comment on various photos. It's such a great discussion piece. It was a simple change, but it had a dramatic style impact. You can do this too! Add photos to your personal space and invest in frames that express your personality.

You can even add fashionable upgrades to uncommon spaces like your car. I removed the de rigueur floor mats in my SUV and ordered custom pink mats with my initials monogrammed on them. How amusing to open a door and be greeted by a shock of pink. If life is a journey, make the ride unforgettable! It is chic, fun and glamorously girly all rolled into one fantastic space. Start staking claim to your personal spaces.

Fashionable living is portable, so take your fashion sense to work with you. I like the sleekest, newest techie toys. When the iPhone came out, I knew instantly I wanted it. I immediately ordered one for my husband and myself. Since they didn't offer a pink version (what were they thinking?), I immediately bought a bright fuchsia cover for personal pizzazz. My digital camera was another tech treat. I was reading a magazine about this new digital camera that was ultra-sleek and small and was all the rage in Japan. To top it off, it came in a gorgeous metallic purple. Sold! I had my personal assistant order it that day. Even my computer mouse is completely covered with Austrian crystals. The little kaleidoscope of color is a simple, but fashionable way to lift my spirits while I work.

> **"Style" is an expression of individualism mixed with charisma. Fashion is something that comes after style.**
> -John Fairchild

My contribution in life is to add color and glamour to all I do and to inspire you to do the same. Whether you opt for cool, modern chrome accessories or go au naturel with rock gardens and bamboo plants, make your workplace your own. Work can be fun if you make your work area look like a fun house. Once again, presentation matters. Invest in matching desk accessories and colored files instead of manila. Buy personalized memo pads instead of the generic kind to add a little pizzazz to your correspondence. If you really want people to pay attention to your memos, use colored ink or stamps. Think of the small splendor of having things at work and home neatly arranged and color-coded. It really is the little things that make fashionable living possible.

## Fashion is a Legacy

Up the ante and turn every daily activity into a moment of élan and style. I put my name or initial on everything, because I believe our name matters. We instill in our children that much like royalty, the Pierce name stands for something special. I began years ago by simply monogramming everyone's towels. Not only does it lend a posh air to an ordinary daily routine, but it instills a sense of worth into my family. Every time they see their name, it makes them think about their life and what it represents. On a sneaky side note, a name on the towel incriminates the person who forgot to clean after themselves, neglecting the household value of neatness and orderliness.

Take home style tips from stately establishments. After many trips to upscale hotels, I noticed they often had a crest or emblem on the toilet paper. That sparked an idea and with a little persistence and research, I had our name embossed on our toilet paper. If you get lost in the house, you can go in the bathroom and be reminded where you are. If hotels can do it, why can't I? It adds a regal touch, and definitely adds a little something to what is usually a pretty unexciting break in the day.

Taste is relative and is the sum total of the intellectual and emotional experiences of the individual. Taste, in order to be positive and vital, must be exercised and developed. A highly cultivated taste, a taste that is knowledgeable and eclectic, is likely to be exciting and provocative, a personal taste at its highest level.
-Eleanor Brown

Think of how you can leave your fashion fingerprint on all you touch today. Stop and meditate on your daily routine and imagine a way that you can upgrade the experience. When you realize life is a collection of experiences, then you can easily think of ways to make it more fashionable and fun. What if when your alarm goes off, it plays music or a pleasant nature sound like rain, instead of an annoying beep? Wouldn't it be better to be soothed awake rather than frightened or annoyed? I personally like to wake up naturally, but that doesn't work for everyone. How about waking to the aroma of freshly brewed coffee each morning, whether you are a coffee drinker or not? Everyone has good associations with the smell of coffee in the morning. It's as simple as purchasing a coffee maker with a timer. Ever think of ending your morning shower wrapped in a warm towel? Towel warmers are easily installed in the bathroom. Anything can receive a new dose of fashion and fun.

## Fashion is a Hunt

Go on a fashion expedition. Find photos of rooms and items that speak to you. When you find a photo, write on that page what struck you about it—was it the color, the placement of the furniture or the lamp in the corner that you noticed? Collect fabric swatches, carpet samples and paint chips that inspire you. Use your Prayer & Purpose Planner to create colorful collages with your goodies. File your clippings away in your Planner pocket for future reference.

Go and explore for inspirational living ideas. Frequent high-end furniture stores; begin to get a taste for how professionals finish a room. As you accumulate these notes and pictures, you will notice a pattern emerging. You may be attracted to the same color range, a certain sofa shape or a particular style of fabric. These are the beginning touchstones of your style. Don't treat this exercise lightly.

Without knowledge, you will waste time and money on the wrong purchases and plans.

When I decorated our current home, I utilized the services of a professional decorator. When we met, I pulled out my binder, where I had collected magazine photos and pictures of places I had traveled to share with her. I had notes of what colors I liked for each room, what initial reactions I had to certain things, etc. This gave her a very good idea of my tastes and the attitude I wanted each room to convey. Her job was just to source the items and crystallize all of my ideas in a harmonious way.

She later told me I was one of the easiest and most entertaining clients to work with. She was impressed that I already had a vision and enough visual aids that it made her job easier. She did not have to decipher my desires; I had a blueprint for her to work from. She noted that my taste level was extremely advanced and could only have come from studying books and visiting hotels and places that utilized haute design. It was one of the best experiences of my life and now I have a home that is really a reflection of me, my family, our values and our lifestyle, instead of a cookie-cutter showroom.

You can do the same for your world. You can use the skills of any designer if you are willing to make the effort to study and plan. It is possible to walk into your home and love being there. You can build a fashionable home and life you enjoy and that represents all the best qualities of you and your family.

> Neither good taste nor wealth, can transform a house into a home, for a home does not consist in the quality of its architecture or decor, but in the quality of the lives that it expresses.
> -Philippa Tristam

## Fashion is a Choice

It is so simple to live fashionably, but it is not always easy. Living fashionably takes observation and work to achieve. It's all based on your personal choice. You will not just wake up one day to better surroundings. You have to decide to make them better. It does not take a lot of money to start. It begins with a few good books, a bag full of design magazines and a Saturday afternoon. Instead of spending a day in front of the TV, watching other people live their great lives, spend time building a collection of idea starters for your new lifestyle. Fashionable living is just a ride to the bookstore away. Bon voyage! See you when you get back!

CREATE A FASHIONABLE LIFE
# Inspiration & Application:

■ A fashionable life is a life well above average. It's an existence watermarked with your values, personal style and quality standards.

■ Fashionable living is learning to run on optimum efficiency, because it is never fashionable to be frazzled.

■ Bring your fashion sense home with you. Incorporate it into your car, china, clothes, décor and personal pursuits.

■ Meditate on your daily routine and imagine a way that you can upgrade the experience.

■ Living fashionably takes observation and work to achieve.

## CHAPTER 6

# CHANGE YOUR THOUGHTS, CHANGE YOUR REALITY

**"A man's life is what his thoughts make of it."**
-Marcus Aurelius

It is our *perception* of the situations in our lives that usually causes us to produce the wrong actions, culminating in wrong results. That trail of wrong perceptions is the catalyst for our depression and frustration, not really the situation at all. You are the change agent for your own life. What you decide to think, ponder and believe produces the results in your life. How you choose to see yourself and your situation determines your destiny. You can spin your life any way you want it; it's all in how you think about things.

The political arena is where the concept of "spin" began. When people in the public eye experience a potentially embarrassing or career damaging moment, they hire media professionals to help put a positive "spin" on it. Spin usually means someone was paid to help reformulate the way we think of something. You may not have a high-priced media guru at your beck and call, but you can learn to do what I call "spin your own record." Make your life a good playlist and stop being a broken record of complaints and sadness. It's as simple as taking what you view as a negative and converting it into a positive.

Package your thoughts differently. See your crisis as an opportunity. Many times we get stuck seeing things a certain way rather than using our mind to see all sides. Stretch your brain to see things differently. You can change your life by changing the way you think.

> Our thoughts create our reality— where we put our focus is the direction we tend to go.
> -Peter McWilliams

Most of us are familiar with the Kennedy family in America as a political and social dynasty. But at one point, the potential destiny and legacy of that family hung in the balance, held hostage by one person's thinking—Rose Fitzgerald Kennedy. In her fifth year of marriage, with three children under age five and pregnant with her fourth, she became frustrated with her life. The repetition of her life as a mother was in stark contrast to the vibrant life she lived as a well-known debutante. Growing frustrated, she ran back home to her parents.

After two weeks, her father helped to change her thinking, and thereby the direction of her life. He jolted her back into reality with these words, "you've made your commitment and you must honor it now. The old days are gone. You can make things work out. If you need more help in the household, then get it. If you need a bigger home, ask for it. If you need more private time for yourself, then take it. There isn't anything you can't do once you set your mind on it. So go now, go back to where you belong."

Her diary notes how that conversation shifted her thinking and strengthened her resolve. She returned home with a purpose that she would not be just a mother, but she would consider herself a teacher, able to put into her children many of the values that she felt made a good human being. She committed herself to educating her children to aspire to higher goals and instilled in them the proper mental skills and values that would make them contributors to this world. When her thoughts toward her life changed, her reality changed. Each day became an opportunity to add value and no longer a chore to endure.

Would we know the name Kennedy if their mother had not changed her focus? In Rose Kennedy's lifetime, mentally challenged people were hidden away, but she insisted that her eldest daughter be a fully included member of the family. The Special Olympics we know today were founded by one of her children, to allow all mentally and physically challenged people the opportunity to be included in sports. The public service they are known for is a result of their mother's personal moral edict from her Catholic upbringing, "to whom much is given, much is required."

What if she had never chosen to change the way she was thinking? Let's bring it a little closer to home. What will happen if you don't change your thinking? Where do you need a new interpretation of your life's events? Your future is what you think of it. It's all a matter of perspective. Shift your thoughts to be success-minded and your life will steer in that direction.

## Think on the Bright Side

As a life coach and mentor, I often have to help people adjust their perspective of their situation. The challenge is helping them see what they do have and taking their focus off what they don't have. I can usually tell that an attitude adjustment is in order when I hear more complaining than celebrating. I know that focus has moved in a negative direction and negativity

**Don't curse the darkness when you can light a candle.**
-Adlai Stevenson

will never produce an inspired lifestyle.  If the direction of your thoughts tend to negativity or depression, your life will remain in the dumps.  Push your way into the positive, by focusing on the light, no matter how dim it may seem.

I refuse to have down days—by choice.  I learned this from my husband, who is never down.  He's steady and consistent, no matter what he faces.  It's not that he doesn't have challenges, because he certainly does.  He just doesn't allow them to keep him tied down or sullen.  He always rises to the top in life because of his choice not to be defeated.  In the end, inspired living is simply a decision.

Don't think with your emotions; think in spite of your emotions. You'll never see your future clearly when your emotions are involved. I realized the truth of this lesson vividly a few years ago.  I purchased exit row seats for a commercial flight I was taking with my husband and children.  My husband and I

> You can never become a great man or woman until you have overcome anxiety, worry, and fear. It is impossible for an anxious person, a worried one, or a fearful one to perceive truth; all things are distorted and thrown out of their proper relations by such mental states, and those who are in them cannot read the thoughts of God.
> -Wallace D. Wattles

were in an exit row and my children were in the seats in front of us.  Upon boarding, the steward gently said we couldn't sit in those seats.  At first I was taken aback.  "Why not?  These are the seats we purchased," I replied.  He went on to explain, "In the event of an emergency, the people sitting in exit rows are supposed to help flight attendants open the exits, and assist others in exiting the plane. As a responsible parent, your first reaction will be to check on your kids in an emergency situation before opening the exit doors, which could jeopardize the safety of all the passengers."  I had to admit it was true. I would follow my heart first and my head later. I graciously took the seats he reassigned us and took away a valuable lesson: Emotional involvement can cause you to override your own better judgment, thus causing you to make bad decisions. Don't allow your emotions to steer your thinking. Feelings are fickle. If you can keep your thoughts focused on succeeding, you'll stay on the course for success.

## You Are What You Think

You will inevitably become what you think about most of the time. Review what is on your mind. Is it problems, or solutions? Is it faith that things are getting better or worse? Think on the bright side! Solomon, the wisest king who ever lived, said, "For as he thinketh in his heart, so is he" (Proverbs 23:7). How true! If you can change your mental meditations, you can change your life. Your thoughts coupled with words are a creative force that will create your reality. You life is like a magnet. You will attract into your life the people, circumstances, ideas and resources in harmony with your dominant thoughts. Think about sickness and you'll feel real (and even imagined) aches and pains. Think healthy thoughts and you'll feel better. Think thoughts of "not enough" and you'll struggle to make ends meet. Change your thinking to abundance and money will flow your way. This is not some New Age mumbo-jumbo but a principle found in the Bible. You are what you think. Change your thinking—change your life!

Changing your thoughts is a lot easier than you think. It's all a matter of developing new thought patterns and getting mentally tough. I'm not talking about doing mental reps to strengthen your frontal lobes, I'm talking about a fresh perspective on life. If you've been breathing bad air created by your own stinking thinking, it's time to change your thoughts and refresh your view. Grasp these rules and get a new mindset and you'll enjoy the sweet smell of success.

# Dr. Stacia's Rules for Rethinking Stinking Thinking:

**RULE #1: Think designer, not discount.** Ladies, let's be honest, wouldn't you rather have Prada pumps over slip-n-slides? A no-brainer, right? That's because when you think of Prada, you think of an elite level of living. A first-class lifestyle starts with luxurious, limitless thoughts. Upgrade your thinking to the highest level. Expect a lot out of life and expect to get it. Don't discount your dreams or count yourself out of the good life. You can have the life you consistently meditate on.

**RULE #2: Think forward, not in reverse.** Your future is not in your past. When driving, there's a reason why your rearview mirror is so small and your windshield is so big. That's because you're supposed to focus on what's on the road ahead and only reference what's behind you quickly. Think forward. Many people get stuck analyzing and apologizing for past mistakes. The milk spilled, now what? No need to cry. Grab a napkin and wipe it up. Simple as that. Your credit card is maxed; work on paying it down. Don't dwell on what went wrong, do something about it. Use your mental energy on thinking and moving forward!

**RULE #3: Rope in unruly thoughts.** When your thoughts start taking on a negative tone, rope them in. Don't allow one negative incident to have free course in your mind and escalate to gargantuan proportions and poison your entire perspective. Maybe you've experienced this before. The thought starts out as "I'm having a bad hair day." Meditated on, it turns into "I hate how I look." This eventually becomes "I hate my job, finances and life." Corral your negative thoughts before they stampede off a cliff into despair. I limit how much consideration I give unpleasant emotions, and then move on so they don't take over my life. I may be sad, mad or upset for 15 minutes, but then I redirect my attention and move on. There's no value in not feeling good. Too much attention to negative thoughts only magnifies the problem and decreases your self-confidence. Ignore them, work toward a solution and their power will dissipate.

**RULE #4: Get inspired thinking through association.** A pity party is simply an invitation to socialize in a pit. That's not my idea of a sensational soiree! I make it my practice to hang out with optimistic others. Rather than seek out others to commiserate with who have unresolved issues like your own, gravitate to the goal-driven who can truly offer you motivation and support. Avoid associates who want to bask in the blues and swap "woe is me" tales. Why settle for empathy when you can have enjoyment? Regain your zest and zeal by hanging around those with their face to the sun. Some rays of joy are bound to fall on you.

**RULE #5: Adopt a "success-or-bust" mentality.** Pure and simple, the inspired in life mentally dwell on the rewards of success. In my mind, failure is not an option. In fact, it rarely enters the equation. It's not that I or success-minded people like me are born with an "optimism gene," but we have changed our thoughts to consider only positive outcomes. Even when things go bad, I view it as an opportunity for the future. When one door closes, seven more are opening ahead. I keep my thoughts along this line even in the midst of a setback. Every delay is in my favor! If you can keep focused on winning, that's exactly what you'll do.

**RULE #6: Stop putting up with thoughts that are holding you back.** Are you tolerating negative self-talk? Sometimes the people who confront others the most put up with the most abusive self-talk from within. You can't keep putting yourself down internally and think you'll rise to the top. Banish the inner critic and instead grab your pompoms and cheer yourself on. A mental pep talk with yourself can rally you more than a session on a shrink's settee. Make a list of five limiting or detrimental thoughts you've told yourself and tolerated for too long. Pay attention to your internal chatter. Whenever one of these thoughts surfaces, say aloud something positive to refute it. Eventually you will retrain your brain to only think the best of yourself.

**RULE #7: Eliminate "if only" thinking.** You have incredible dreams and goals, but *if only* you had the money, *if only* you didn't have kids, *if only* you had the education, *if only* you were single, *if only* you lived in a bigger city or a bigger house, *if only* you were more motivated, well…you could succeed. "If only" thinking means you dream inspired but think negatively. This is quite self-defeating. Stop paying lip-service to what you want and go for it! Take one little step…just one! If you rest on your "if only," you'll live a second-rate life. You have the ability to live the life you want if you'll take a step in the right direction. You can do it! My son wrote his own book on the matter titled, *"If You Think You Can You Can, If You Think You Can't You Can't."* Most adults can benefit from this quick read!

**RULE #8: Deliberately speak only good things for the next 30 days.** This is when the going will get tough if you've been a negative thinker for long. For an entire 30 days you can only speak positive things. Speak positively about absolutely everything—your children, your job, your co-worker, that new assignment you were given unexpectedly, your money and even the weather. Your words have creative power. You will manifest the life you constantly think and speak of. At first, it will sound as if you're talking unrealistically. But soon you will find out what was formerly "realistic" was really just negative. At the end of the exercise, either you'll talk a lot less or you'll retrain yourself to think positive so you can speak positive. Either way, it's a win for you!

**RULE #9: Pray your way into inspired thinking.** Morning prayer will ease your mind and cause you to make more accurate decisions during the day. Prayer makes you a more positive, inspired and grateful person, which will yield you lots of successful results. Try setting aside 20 minutes each morning to pray and meditate on all that is good in your life. Focus on how you want your day to turn out and see it! Then get moving. Watch how in 30 days, your thinking will be transformed and you will be able to testify of the outstanding and good things happening to you all the time.

**RULE #10: Love the fight as much as the finish.** View each day as another opportunity to think your best thoughts and live your best life. Fight to improve yourself, even if it's only by increments. Love the progress you're making and the changes, no matter how small. It's the fight you can control, so stay focused on how much you love seeing what you're made of. If you do this, your finish will be phenomenal!

## Own Up, So You Can Think Higher

You will never change your thoughts without really being honest. You are the result of your choices. You may have had some hard knocks; you may have started life with a detriment, but today is your day of reckoning. No matter what, you are what you are and that is what you will be until you assume responsibility for it and make a decision to change. The decision is in your hands. You can blame the world or change your world, but you won't be able to do both at the same time. Admit to your reality. You will never be able to conquer what you will not confront, and ignorance is not inspiring. Ostriches put their head in the sand to avoid trouble, and you, my friend, are no ostrich! Lift up your head, grab your couture ostrich flight case and think higher so you can begin to fly with us eagles—the view is much better from up here!

CHANGE YOUR THOUGHTS,
CHANGE YOUR REALITY

## Inspiration & Application:

■ What you decide to think, ponder and believe produces the results in your life.

■ Package your thoughts differently. See your crisis as an opportunity.

■ You'll never see your future clearly when your emotions are involved.

■ You will attract into your life the people, circumstances, ideas and resources in harmony with your dominant thoughts.

■ To change your thoughts, you must develop new thought patterns and get mentally tough.

## CHAPTER 7

# ADMIT WHEN YOU'RE NOT GOOD AT SOMETHING AND EITHER GIVE IT UP OR GET SOME HELP

**"If at first you don't succeed, get help or quit!"**
**-Dr. Stacia Pierce**

Contrary to the old euphemism, I believe that quitters win and winners quit or else they call for help—it's all about knowing when each decision is appropriate. Understanding when to hold 'em and when to fold 'em is one of the best principles in life you can master. I'm a champion at persistence and endurance, and I don't like throwing in the towel. I believe an undefeatable attitude is vital to succeed in business and your personal life, but I also believe in exercising *all* my options to win—two of my options being getting help or quitting. Getting help doesn't mean you're weak and quitting doesn't make you a failure. Both are valuable choices when exercised at the proper time.

Many times I see people operating with tunnel vision. They are failing in an endeavor but refuse to get help or quit. Their pride launches them into hero mode, making them even more determined to "make it work," all the while embarrassed that it isn't already so. That's maddening. Albert Einstein said it best, "Insanity: doing the same thing over and over again and expecting different results."

At some point you have to know when to call it quits and move on to fight another battle. Here's my philosophy: figure out how to fly fast or fail fast so you can either get help or quit and move on. You always have choices! It's good to have a "tackle the world" mentality to aid you when winning through sheer effort is the only

**Of all the stratagems, to know when to quit is the best.**
-Chinese Proverb

alternative, but in most situations, there is a smarter, more effective way of doing things. In short, if you are struggling with something, there usually *is* an easier way. The hardest part is often simply acknowledging it.

## Quit When It's Not Working

Knowing when it's time to quit and when it's time to call for help comes down to having a good understanding of timing. You should give up when you're totally failing at something. Sometimes I see people who have a business idea that's not working. They keep pushing but wisdom is telling them that this is not a good idea. No matter how much they push, they still never get a break. Wise others are telling them to do something different, but they refuse to listen. Don't go through life so headstrong that you won't give up on an idea that keeps turning out wrong. There's a certain grace that comes with your course. When you're in the pathway of God's plan, there will be divine "breaks" and entryways into success. Now, I'm not saying every time you encounter resistance on the road to your dream, you should stop. There *is* a fight on the road to success, but there should also be proof and evidence along the way that you're on course. Quit when it's obvious you are off track.

## Quit When It's Time to Change

Sometimes you will need to quit even when you are on the right course in life, because it's time to change directions. I can remember when I was passionate about business and beauty and owned my own makeup salon in an upscale mall. At the time, that was my focus and drive. When I married my husband a couple of years later, I knew he was called to ministry. Within our first year of marriage, I kept the business going but I was feeling like it was time to change directions. Shortly after, my husband and I were sent to Lansing to start a ministry and it was time let the store go. I called it quits on the business and instead brought all my business sense and love for image to ministry. Now, I still get to do what I love but on God's course for my life, not my own. You have to know when it's time to let something go and change lanes.

## Quit When You'll Lose More Than You'll Gain

No one likes to concede defeat and chalk something up as a loss, but sometimes it is in your best interest to quit. Most gamblers who experience monstrous losses suffer from this plight. They continue to call when they are clearly beat, refusing to admit defeat or they "chase their losses" thinking if they gamble more, they will eventually get their money back. Soon a little loss turns into huge deficits.

You're probably not in this extreme bunch, but you may have suffered from a "non-quitting" mentality before. Have you ever tried to justify a mistake by throwing more resources at it? Perhaps you went shopping and made an impulse buy—a shirt. The shirt cost you too much to begin with, but you felt liberal and decided to go for the splurge. When you got home, you realized the shirt went with absolutely nothing in your closet. Rather than quit and admit your folly, you went out and bought shoes, pants and accessories to go with it, spending even more money, to justify the original purchase. That's simply throwing good money away or what economists call "the sunk cost fallacy." Sometimes it's better to just quit while you're ahead and think of the money lost as a lesson learned. Know your limits and know when to let something go or bow out gracefully. You may not be able to recoup your losses, but you don't have to dig yourself in any further. Remember, you're playing to win the whole game of life, not just one hand.

Now that you know when to quit, here's my word of caution. Never quit just because you don't feel like doing something. Quitting is a solution that should be exercised with discernment, not reckless abandon. Remember what I said earlier, you have options! Quitting is only one of them. Sometimes you need to go with Option B—

**Humility is to make a right estimate of one's self.**
-Charles Haddon Spurgeon

getting help! It's not that you need to give it up, you just need a helping hand from a more knowledgeable, skilled person in order to succeed. Start by admitting it!

## Help Wanted

So you're not good at everything? Welcome to the human race. No one is. God designed us so we would be interdependent and need one another. No one is good at everything, but everyone is good at something. The first step is admitting you are not the second coming of the Savior. Sounds funny, but many women need this reminder. Pride can cause you to lose your perspective. It locks you into thinking you need to master everything. You wind up spending your days in a personal prison of proving to everyone that you're a pro. This is a very unrealistic and ineffective way to live. Being able to admit you're not good at something and reaching out for a helping hand is a sign of humility. This attitude opens you up to see multiple methods and creative sources for achieving your goals. If you were brutally honest, you'd admit that not only are you not good at everything, you don't even *want to be* good at everything. I know there are just some things I'm not interested in (and probably never will be) and I'm glad I can pay someone else to be good at it who really enjoys it. I believe in capitalizing on my strengths and staffing my weaknesses. I get help whenever needed and as often as I can.

**Focus on your forte, not your frustrations.**
-Dr. Stacia Pierce

## Team Up

We've all been in over our heads at one time or another and it's no big deal to call out for a little help now and again. Whether it's losing weight, eliminating debt, starting a business or launching a women's ministry, your success is multiplied when you ask someone who's already successful in that area for help.

Learn to collaborate. When you draw on the strengths of others, you exponentially increase your success factor. The truth is that to be really effective in today's world, you need to rely on a whole team of people, both inside and outside your network. There's no way I can know everything there is to know about everything. That's why I build great relationships and great teams so I have experts to call on when necessary.

## From Hairpins to Hired Help

I remember a time when this lesson transformed my business. At the time, I was a 20-something entrepreneur with dreams and ambitions the size of Texas. I had purchased a salon, hired six stylists and experienced moderate success. However, not being a former stylist, I didn't always understand the business from an operational side, which limited my success. There was always inventory to be ordered, payroll and accounting duties, salon maintenance and a whole host of other responsibilities. Although it was sensible to do as much of this as possible when launching the business, the business had grown and I had built a profitable venture. If I wanted to expand to a new level, I had to admit I needed expert help. I recruited and hired a top person in the salon business. As soon as I turned the operational side over to her, the salon exploded and business boomed. It continued to expand and I eventually added on a barber shop and conglomerate of other businesses. Had I not asked for help, I would have been hung up on how many hairpins to order rather than focused on what I was good at—guiding top-level management and overseeing the strategic direction of the company.

I'm here to let you in on a little secret: Asking for help is liberating! It frees you to be true to yourself and gives someone else in the world, who is gifted in that area, a chance to shine and help you look good. Why insist a square peg fit in a round hole? I simply admit the obvious and move on. I'm not great at web design. Rather than use all my free time trying to master mediocrity at best, I am able to direct my energies at being an exceptional boss and hiring someone who is great at building websites. Being a know-it-all is unrealistic and inefficient. I'd rather be a hire-it-all. Spreading what you're not good at with experts in certain areas, such as bookkeeping, legal support and distribution and marketing, for example, means you get to devote more time to your own areas of expertise. This is smart in business and in your personal life. Do you labor over laundry? Get help! Does going to the dentist for a root canal sound more desirable than clearing the clutter in your basement? Get help! Does the U.S. government have a better chance of balancing the fiscal budget than you do of balancing your checkbook? Get help!

You'd be amazed to find out how many people would be overjoyed and willing to help out. Your problem could be someone else's passion. I recently learned this lesson. I was at home going through my digital pictures and realized that I had a lot of pictures that needed to be placed in albums, however, I didn't want them arranged in any old way. I wanted them organized and scrapbooked in a memorable way. As busy as I was, I knew this would be a project I would probably never get around to and would be a source of frustration left undone. An idea struck me to ask for help from one of the ladies I mentor. She loved photography and scrapbooking, and it would solve a problem for me while providing extra income for her, while she did something she was passionate about. She was delighted by the offer and we struck a mutually beneficial agreement. Think about your home, family and job. Where do you need help? Who do you know who is passionate about that? Can you hire help? If not, who do you know who would do it for the experience? Think creatively and you will find the help you need.

## Helpful Hints When Getting Help

**1. Get help early.** If you're constantly frustrated or completely stuck, it's time to call in the troops. Still hesitant? Think about the consequences of not asking for help.

**2. Don't wait until it's too late.** Ask for help as soon as you think you might need it so you can resolve your current issue in a timely manner or even stop an issue before it becomes a major problem.

**3. Be specific.** Determine what you need help with and present a clear picture of the outcome you desire. Be as detailed as possible. This will make it easier for everyone involved.

**4. Be willing to buy or barter for help.** If you can hire help outright, I highly recommend it. You will get a professional who can tackle what you can't. However, if you're not in a position to pay for services, consider bartering what you do well for another's talent. If you enjoy cooking, double your menu and swap dinner delivery for cleaning services. Be resourceful. I know a woman who wanted to use her basement as a place for exercise and quiet meditation. Not wanting to rack up a bill replacing the carpeting, she bartered with the owner of a flooring store and struck a great deal. She would tutor his third-grade son in math and reading in exchange for new carpet installation. Get creative.

**5. Don't be a silent martyr.** Suffering in silence only hurts you. No one can read your mind, so you must speak up if you're going to get the help you need.

Sometimes in our homes, we're not happy with the way things are running but we haven't voiced our concerns. Don't suffer in silence. Ask for help. I am fortunate to have a lot of hired help in my home, but this was not always the case. I can remember when the demands of ministry were eclipsing my duties at home and it became a huge challenge to keep both running at the level of excellence I was used to. I remember getting alone and praying, asking God to send people to help me. Within a couple of weeks, one of the young ladies I mentored came up to me after a Sunday morning service and volunteered to clean my home every week. Eventually she became one of my hired staff. As the relationship grew, I even mentored her in the launch of her own cleaning business and helped guide her through hiring employees and negotiating several huge cleaning contracts. All this came as a result of my simple prayer for help and her willingness to be a help.

When you are on God's path to success, there are people assigned to help you succeed in life and people whom you are called to help. Be open to both. When you're willing to lend a hand to others, then you will have no qualms in asking for the assistance you need. Someone is waiting in the wings to step up and assist. It's the Law of Reciprocity in action. Admit when you're not good at something and get the help you need! And if all else fails, quit and keep moving forward toward success!

ADMIT WHEN YOU'RE NOT
GOOD AT SOMETHING...

## Inspiration & Application:

■ **Getting help doesn't mean you're weak and quitting doesn't make you a failure. Both are viable choices when exercised at the proper time.**

■ **If you are struggling with something, there usually *is* an easier way.**

■ **Quit when it's not working, when it's time to change directions or when you'll lose more than you'll gain.**

■ **When you get help and draw on the strengths of others, you exponentially increase your success factor.**

■ **When you are on God's path to success, there are people assigned to help you succeed in life and people whom you are called to help.**

## CHAPTER 8

# BLEND LIFE AND WORK, THEN YOU'LL HAVE BALANCE

**"If you nurture your mind, body, and spirit, your time will expand.
You will gain a new perspective that will allow you to accomplish much more."
-Brian Koslow**

I love the thrill of pursuit that each day has to offer. There have been so many technological advances that you can now connect with anyone in the world at any time. Rather than find this 24/7-paced life invasive, I find it empowering. There's a world of opportunities at my doorstep. Each day, I wake up excited to capitalize on the possibilities life has to offer. While I wish I was in the vast majority, it's sad to say that most people feel overburdened by life rather than uplifted. Facing multiple demands, they often ask me, "How do you find balance with work and life?" To which I reply, "I don't. I blend the two."

I've always lived my life by the philosophy that the success of my work contributes to the success of my family, and the success of my family contributes to the success of my work. I never make myself choose between the two—I choose both! Don't think of work and life as two opposing ends on a scale where one side's gain is the other side's loss, but rather…a pie—a portfolio of choices that are all worthy of investing in. Family, friends, career, ministry, health, finances—these are all worthy pursuits and all of these make up a whole, satisfying life.

The idea of separating the two implies that your life's work is something you are trying to get through so you can go home and do what you really enjoy. That's not my reality and it shouldn't be yours. You should enjoy and relish every aspect of your life. Don't be misguided by those who say that the secret to balance is to find more hours in a day by cutting back on work or family and living happier with less. I don't believe that. Less is just that…less. In real life, success is a combination of blending achievement and enjoyment in *all* areas of your life. When you blend work and life, you get the most out of both. That's balance. Girlfriend, it's time to get a new mindset. Rather than itemizing your hours into separate categories, look at every moment as contributing to a wholly satisfying life.

Successfully blending work and life requires commitment, passion— and to be honest—a lot of time and effort. Most successful people don't just work hard at work. You have to use your same creativity, diligence, passion and drive to have a thriving family as well. Some days, I just have to do it all. I may attend one of my son's gymnastic meets later in the evening and still come home, work out and write my next message for Bible study. On those days, I have a "whatever it takes" approach and push it out. Other times, I have to forgo my down time to meet a pressing deadline. You must continually evaluate your priorities and make tradeoffs. Contentment comes from happy compromises. I've decided to embrace this fact and make it work in the best interests of my life and family.

For example, at the time of this writing, I've planned my son's upcoming birthday party, teleconferenced with my staff, negotiated some business transactions over the phone, wrote this chapter, worked out to my exercise video and updated my blog on my weight loss website, **www.mydreamweight.ws**. All of these activities took different amounts of time, but they all were important so they all got done. All in a day's work at my house (and I still plan to squeeze in some shopping later this evening). My life is full of multiple roles and responsibilities, but I never consider any of them interruptions. I love being a wife, mother, co-pastor, mentor, television personality, entrepreneur, author, itinerant speaker, philanthropist, web show host…and the list goes on. I do all of this and yet feel very balanced. Does everything in my life get equal attention? No. However, I blend all these aspects of myself together so that I'm not feeling pulled in 10 different directions.

## Recipe for Success

**If you are truly flexible and go until... there is really very little you can't accomplish in your lifetime.**
-Anthony Robbins

Life is meant to be fluid. Every activity doesn't require the same attention as the next and different roles take priority in life during different seasons. Like baking a cake, you must gather all the ingredients of a successful life and blend them together until you have a winning recipe for a satisfying life. The ingredients that work for you and how much of them you need depend on your lifestyle tastes, preferences and priorities. Add in a pinch more of this, scale back on a little of that, until it all blends just right. At a different stage of your life, you might mix the ingredients differently and come up with a totally new recipe that still tastes great. Life is inventive like that, so adopt an attitude of flexibility.

## Get a Panoramic Perspective

Focus on enjoying and achieving something in every single area of your life. Refuse to settle for the status quo. You can do, be, have, achieve and become more than you think. God put so much ingenuity, creativity and resourcefulness inside you, but most people never tap into all their potential to create a dream life. What would you want your life to look like if you silenced all the limiting thoughts and believed you could have it all? What would a thriving family, dynamic spiritual walk and booming business look like blended together? Now, add in a life of perfect health, thriving children, a sizzling marriage and financial security and independence.

Starting to get the picture? This can be your reality but you first must believe the blended life is possible.

My Prayer & Purpose Planner can help you dream, achieve and blend the life you desire. The Planner is a tool that contains a dream diary for you to pen your priorities, evaluate your values and script your desires. It continually prompts you to gather magazines and cut out pictures, words and phrases that bring your dreams to life. I have filled my Prayer & Purpose Planner with pages depicting my children's success, health goals, business and ministry projects, family and fortune. Looking at these pages allows me to see the end from the beginning and make daily choices that align with my deepest desires. Because I have a picture of it all, I see creative solutions to be successful in every area and make it work together. When you find that you are juggling priorities and face competing demands, it's usually because you've lost sight of the big picture and forgotten that God designed it all to work together and work out for your good.

Have you ever taken a picture and zoomed in so much that you unintentionally cut someone's head or arm out of the photo? That's how many of us operate in life. We've focused in so much on the day-to-day details that we've unintentionally cut out something essential to our life's perfect picture. Zoom out and widen your frame of reference. Take a panoramic perspective of life and you will capture new inspirations and solutions for living. Think big and think blended and you'll make everything fit again.

Once you've made the mental shift to a bountiful, blended life, you're ready for some practical how-tos to make this all work. There are some practical things you can do that will help everything gel together much easier. Here are my fab five habits that, if applied to your work and your life, will lead you to blended bliss.

## 1. Make Your Passion Your Play

When you love what you do, it doesn't feel like work. A big reason most women want to separate work from life is they have lost the joy in what they do. You might not be working your dream job, but you can love the work you do. Take pride in a job done well by doing your personal best every day. Don't fight work. See it as your chance to perfect your skills, hone your work ethic and become an expert. All of these traits add value to your other roles, whether parent, entrepreneur, philanthropist or wife.

## 2. Prioritize Parenting

Whenever possible, I include my family in my professional life. My husband and I involve our children in our entrepreneurial endeavors. This allows me to spend time with them while working and it also teaches my children a valuable lesson about entrepreneurship.

Everyone in our family has businesses they oversee and manage.

■   My husband and I have started a ministry travel company (**www.lifechangerstravel.com**) and I have my own line of fragrance and accessories (**www.styleshoppe.com**).

■   My son has a line of smart clothing and hip thinking caps for boys, called Boy Brilliance (**www.boybrilliance.com**).

■   My daughter's business, The Billionheir Girls Club, features her own line of preppy clothes, accessories, DVDs and girly growth tools (**www.billionheirgirlsclub.com**).

As a family we strategize, forecast and plan market expansion and commercial shoots.  It's fun to work and play together.

As part of the first family of Life Changers Christian Center, my children play a huge role in our ministry endeavors.  I bring my children on my web show and periodically feature them as special guests at Successful Living Bible Study.  One of our biggest events was The Pierce Family Book Review, in which our whole family shared the inspiration behind the books we have written and why reading is such an important legacy in our family life.  Seeing how important my family is to me helps women across the country who watch the broadcast make a bridge between their own family and work.  Ladies, I'm here to tell you that it is possible to have a thriving career and family if you're willing to blend the two.

## 3.  Make Room for Romance

With work schedules, routines and children, you must have a plan if you're going to keep your marriage poppin'. Because my husband and I pastor Life Changers Christian Center, we have the great fun of working together.  To avoid the tension of overlapping commitments, communication becomes ultra-important. We talk all the time, which creates a tremendous level of intimacy in our relationship. Because Sunday is such a power-packed day with my husband flying between our church locations and ministering multiple times, we usually reserve Mondays as our chance to take time out and get into each other. We share dreams, plan for our future and family and of course, have plenty of romance to keep our relationship sizzling hot. We truly are partners from the bedroom to the boardroom.

**Work together to create a plan that will allow you and your spouse to look forward to spending the rest of your lives together happily married.**
-Steve Harley

Whether you work with your spouse or not, you should see your spouse as your partner and purpose to be his greatest cheerleader. Spend time talking with him and sharing each other's dreams. Discuss ways to better please each other in and out of the boudoir and become an expert at it. Make your marriage and romance an integral part of every area of your life and you'll find a great deal more balance and bliss.

## 4. Delight in the Details

Part of successfully blending all areas of your life is a matter of getting organized. Keeping a calendar is a great tool to see your month at a glance. Because my household operates like an airport, with someone coming and going at all times of the day, it is vital that I put all of our family's important dates on one central calendar so I can see how they all fit together. I include things like family vacations, speaking engagements, business trips, birthdays, anniversaries, date nights, ministry functions, shopping trips, holidays and my children's programs and activities at school. Everything is important, so we make it all work by planning out the details.

Once the dates are set, I plan out the details of each event in my day planner. My planner looks more like a transcription tape than a loose list, because I fill it with written notes down to the smaller detail. I can run my whole life by my day planner. In it I have the following:

- My wardrobe shopping list for the upcoming season
- Pictures of shoes, clothes and accessories I need to order from stores or items I'm on the waiting list for
- My travel itinerary for the year
- Dates of my mentor's anniversaries, birthdays and gift ideas for each of them
- A list of my family vacations, complete with hotel, car rental and flight information
- A list of faith projects and dream items that I'm believing God for
- My financial plan—what I am planning on sowing for the year as well as what I need to earn monthly, daily and hourly
- Confessions for every area of my life
- My goals for the year
- My reading list (books I want to buy)

Having plans on paper helps me to have a big-picture view and properly execute so that everything turns out successfully. Delighting in the details also helps me to be flexible and fluid in the moment when the unexpected happens. A project may take longer than I thought or something great like a new opportunity may open up unexpectedly. Either way, I can make it work and adjust to ever-changing circumstances and new responsibilities when I already have a written plan in place. If you're overwhelmed with any aspect of your life, it's a sign that you lack organization in that area. Organization always brings solutions, clarity and focus.

Take time out right now to get organized. Create a list of planning tools you need to add order to your life. Schedule some events on your calendar. Put your thoughts on paper by journalizing creative solutions to add order to your life. A well-blended, inspired life begins with a plan!

## 5. Hang Up Your Halo

Just when you've found a perfect balance that works for you and you're ready to shine your halo and fluff your wings, your season of life will inevitably change and you will have to rebalance everything all over again. You get married. You open a new business after being a stay-at-home mom for years. You have twins. Wherever your path leads, learn how to shift when needed. Make life and work happen on your terms. There's no one cookie-cutter mold you have to fit into. I'll let you in on a little secret. No one is perfect. Life is not perfect. So take the pressure off of yourself. Lose that all-or-nothing mentality. Refuse to think that if everything is not going perfectly in every single area, then nothing is going right. Find spots of balance and moments of joy and relish in those.

Things may go a bit haywire one day. I also have those days, but I laugh and enjoy the challenge of having a great day in spite of it all. It's in these moments that I grow the most as a person and discover untapped talents. The key to finding and maintaining balance is to continually be open to learn, grow and change along the way. If you adapt these lifestyle habits and take a broader, more blended view of your roles and responsibilities, you will become the picture of success you once envisioned. Say cheese!

### BLEND LIFE AND WORK, THEN YOU'LL HAVE BALANCE

# Inspiration & Application:

■ Don't think of work and life as two opposing ends on a scale where one side's gain is the other side's loss, but rather…a pie—a portfolio of choices that are all worthy of investing in.

■ Life is meant to be fluid.

■ Whenever possible, include your family in your professional life.

■ Make your marriage and romance an integral part of every area of your life and you'll find a great deal more balance and bliss.

■ If you're overwhelmed with any aspect of your life, it's a sign that you lack organization in that area.

## CHAPTER 9

# DO SOMETHING FUN
# FOR YOURSELF EVERY WEEK

**"He who does not get fun and enjoyment
out of every day needs to reorganize his life."
-George Matthew Adams**

We all need time to do something we *really* find fun. As adults, most of us are fun-deprived and it shows in our zeal for life. Many women just end up going through the motions and losing sight of what really energizes them. Sometimes what you lack in motivation is not physical. It's not that we haven't had enough sleep or haven't exercised. It's that you haven't done anything *truly* fun in a long, long time. Having fun gives you emotional energy. Fun creates a sense of vitality of mind and spirit that reconnects you to the joy of life.

Have you become so beleaguered with problems and circumstances that you've forgotten life is fun and meant to be enjoyed? Girls, the good life is a fun-filled life. You need not plan an elaborate Riviera cruise or have the money to buy Manolos to have a little fun. All you need is a sense of adventure and a willingness to explore a bit. There are fun discoveries you can make in your own city. Visit a historical site, enjoy patronizing local art shops or drive through an upscale neighborhood and dream.

One of my favorite fun spots is the bookstore. My family and I make a day out of it. We treat ourselves to Starbucks, load up on books and leisurely stroll the aisles. It's such a simple treat and an easy way to rejuvenate. You can have fun without spending a lot; you just need to be creative and enjoy the moments in each day. Studies show that people who are able to find enjoyment in daily pleasures are naturally more optimistic and resilient when handling real crises. These people tend to see the good in bad situations and find the silver lining in every cloud. Their spirit has been nourished through daily amusement, so when trouble hits, they can "take a licking and keep on ticking." I always purpose to see negative circumstances as temporary. I choose to believe there is always a fun-filled opportunity waiting for me around the next bend and because I expect it, that's exactly what I find.

## Laugh It Up

One of the biggest parts of having fun in life has to do with your attitude. Learn to lighten up. Laugh a lot. Fun, humor and a good dash of delight have been shown to alleviate depression and fight disease. One study showed that cancer patients who incorporated laughter into their treatments by watching funny sitcoms recovered faster than other cancer patients. King Solomon once said, "A merry heart doeth good like a medicine: but a broken spirit drieth the bones" (Proverbs 17:22). When was the last time you exercised your funny bone?

> **A day without laughter is a day wasted.**
> -Charlie Chaplin

My family and I always find occasion to laugh each and every day. As the first family of a major ministry, there are always problems and challenges that come our way. Yet we don't take all of this pressure home and make everything a serious issue for our family. We enjoy ministry and so do our children. Even at church, our members have adopted this celebratory mentality. We smile and cheer and get excited about the Word. The atmosphere is filled with joy and excitement. My husband and I have built a contemporary ministry that attracts the unchurched. People are attracted because we incorporate elements of fun throughout the ministry with performing arts, world-class guest speakers and entertainers and even some comedic performances from my husband when he's making a funny point in his message.

When we started in ministry, we decided to teach the Word in a fun, relevant manner and we have kept that philosophy central to the vision. In fact, I decided to put a fun, new twist on the International Women's Success Conference this year. Being that I love laughter and infusing women's lives with enjoyment, I decided to launch an online comedy contest that would conclude at my women's conference. Any female around the country who thought she was funny could enter by submitting a two-minute video to YouTube of herself performing original comedy. The idea was a huge hit. Entries poured in from around the country. I found out there were many funny ladies right in our own congregation as well. The winner of the contest won a huge cash prize, a promotional package and a chance to perform live at the International Women's Success Conference, attended by more than 4,000 women and 600 teens from across the nation. The entire contest was a huge success.

**Fun is about as good a habit as there is.**
-Jimmy Buffet

I got so many emails from other leading ladies around the country, thanking me for being so innovative and bringing the love of laughter to the body of Christ. It's good to have fun!

Fun is necessary! You'll miss something vital on the path to an inspired life without it. Live a thrilling life, but don't wait for someone else to add in the fun factor. You must do something fun for yourself! What is fun for one person differs from the next. If taking an art class doesn't appeal to you, maybe traveling abroad or attending a Broadway play is more your style. Do the things you like to do. Engage in your form of fun. I love to shop and I make no apologies about it. It doesn't matter whether I'm in an upscale mall or my local Target, I love the thrill of the hunt that shopping affords. Because this is my passion, I make time for it. It doesn't matter how busy I get, I always add in a little shopping to my week. Take time to do something you enjoy each week.

## Factor In Family Fun

No matter how hectic your schedule or large your family, you have time for fun! You just have to seize the moments. It's worth it and it makes life so much more rewarding. When my husband and I recently went to Houston for a whirlwind three-day weekend, I learned just how much you could get done in a day. I flew in to do a women's conference. I ministered three times. I met and dined with the conference host. Then my husband and I met with another pastor and his wife who live in a suburb of Houston. Later that night, my husband and I were picked up by limousine for a dinner meeting with our mentors, who gave us valuable business advice. During all this, I managed to squeeze in lots of shopping, dine at a new restaurant and enjoy a little pampering while getting my nails done. I refused to go all the way across the country and not enjoy some fun while I was there.

That's how you have to be—adamant to squeeze the joy out of every experience and every moment. Get creative. Make time for fun! Schedule fun time into your week. You should have time for fun alone and time for fun with others. Plan regular date nights with your spouse and fun nights with the kids. Having fun together is not optional. Fun time is the glue of intimacy.

Have fun trying new things together. Even fun can get stale if you always do the same activities. Mix it up a bit. Instead of going to the movies, go to see a Broadway show. Take up backpacking. Try an art class. Here's my challenge to you: If it's something you wouldn't ordinarily do, do it. Try a cuisine you've never eaten. Take a new route on your way home. Read a magazine you wouldn't ordinarily pick up. You'll discover that new experiences, no matter how small, will revive your spontaneity and spunk.

Right now, create a Fun File. Grab a file folder and a piece of paper. On your note paper, write the heading, "My Fun Favorites." Then list 25 fun things you love to do or would love to try. Include fun people you would enjoy on an adventure, fun books you want to read, movies and performances to see and vacation spots that would add fun to your life. Use the next 30 days to incorporate as many of the items as possible off your list into your life. For the really big items, start hunting and gathering information and brochures and keep them in your Fun File.

Reclaim your joie de vivre. Don't wait for someone to give you permission to indulge in the things you love. Joy, self-care and bouts of play are key to a well-lived life. Think of this as your permission slip!

DO SOMETHING FUN
FOR YOURSELF EVERY WEEK

## Inspiration & Application:

■ Fun creates a sense of vitality of mind and spirit that reconnects you to the joy of life.

■ Having fun in life centers on your attitude. Learn to lighten up and laugh a lot.

■ Don't wait for someone else to add in the fun factor. You must do something fun for yourself each week!

■ No matter how hectic your schedule or large your family, you have time for fun! You just have to seize the moments.

■ Have fun trying new things together. Even fun can get stale if you always do the same activities.

## CHAPTER 10

# KNOW WHEN IT'S TIME TO GET OUT OF THE BATTLE AND GO TO WAR

**"Let him who desires peace prepare for war."**
**-Flavius Vegetius Renatus**

For the past couple of years, I've been battling to lose weight. I would face choices daily as to what I would eat, how much and be the consequences of it all. More times than not, I was winning the battle, but it all seemed uphill. While writing in my journal one morning, I remember writing these words, "God, why is losing weight such a battle? I'm ready to win already." A reply came to my spirit just as clear as day—a simple statement: "It's because you haven't decided it's time to get out of the battle and go to war." As I pondered these words, a newfound revelation came to me. I had been battling with weight, unsure that I really had it in me to win. I never really locked in on my goal and internally insisted that my mind, body and spirit come in line with my decision. Because I had not made a definitive decision that I was going to win no matter what, I kept battling back and forth. I had never settled the issue and declared myself bigger than my problem.

Even in the dictionary, there is a defining difference between being in a battle and war. Webster's defines a battle as "a controversy or struggle between two parties." A war is "a concerted effort to end the debate and settle the matter." Battles can be ongoing. When it comes to declaring war, a line has been drawn in the sand and the words "no more" are uttered. An ultimatum has been given, and now it's time to rally resources, conquer and conclude the matter. War may sound like a harsh word, but I define it simply as deciding to make an all-out effort to achieve your God-given goals in spite of opposition.

With my newfound understanding, I declared war! I was going to war on weight loss and this time I was winning. I insisted to myself that I really meant business and I was going to achieve my goal. No more would I look at the obstacles as worthy opponents who could determine daily whether I would advance or retreat. I decided conclusively that every day I was going to take a little step forward, and then another, until I completely won and reached my dream weight and developed a healthier lifestyle.

Since making that decision, the struggle has been over. I still have to make diligent effort, but the feeling of battling is gone. I'm determined. I win. That's it. What in your life do you need to get out of the battle and go to war on? What has kept you defeated that you need to conquer? What daunting decisions or uncertainties are you battling? Make a list. Draft a declaration of war. Even countries do this before taking an aggressive course of action. Writing down your intentions strengthens your resolve and defines your commitment to succeed in spite of resistance. This is the first step to victory.

> It is fatal to enter any war without the will to win it.
> -General Douglas MacArthur

## From Kid's Games to Grown-Up Goals

I remember as a kid one of my favorite childhood card games was "War." There was something about facing off with matching cards and uttering the words "I declare war" to see whose next card would be the highest and win the prize. It's not that I was ultra-competitive in the sense that I enjoyed striving to beat my friends and family; I just enjoyed the challenge of winning when the odds were great. Of course, with cards, it was all a matter of luck whether I won or lost, but not so in life. Winning or losing in life is all a matter of the choices you make and sometimes you still have to declare war. Girlfriend, repeat after me: "I declare war on debt! I declare war on sickness! I declare war on anything that stands in the way of God's best for my life!" Sometimes all you need to do to overcome a negative situation is declare war. This simply means speaking aloud your right to victory and mustering all your resources to win. When bills face off with you, declare war! When bad relationships chase you down, declare war! Settle for nothing less than obtaining the good life God promised you.

## Count Up the Cost and Devise a Battle Plan

Once war has been declared, you must plan out your strategy for victory. Now that you know what it is you want to achieve, you must count up how much it's going to cost you. When I wanted to lose weight, I knew it would cost me time, effort and focus. I had to invest in new workout videos and clothes to keep myself motivated. I had to invest in better snacks and healthier groceries. I had to buy books and gain more knowledge of how to live healthier. It cost me to achieve, but it was worth the price. Sometimes we want things too easily and we haven't added up what it will cost us and whether we are willing to pay the price. Take a minute to write down five things you will have to do, buy, become or invest in order to reach your goal. Now come up with a strategy to get it done. Write down several concrete action steps you will take. Set deadlines for yourself. Put your plans on your monthly calendar. Make your strategy as detailed as possible so you can move quickly into action mode. Settle on a definitive course of action and stick to it. With plans in place, you're ready to get started.

## Develop a Fighting Spirit

To see your life as God sees it, you must be willing to put up a fight. There will always be resistance on the path to success. Problems can attack you and so can people. Sometimes the resistance is even internal. It's that little harassing voice of doubt that says "you'll never succeed" or "you've tried before and failed and this time will be no different." That's when you need your fighting spirit. There comes a time when you have to stand up and fight and back down the situation with a bold declaration of war. When you refuse to cower to the opposition, what once intimidated you will recede. Get tough. Too many times I see ladies settle for less in life because of negative circumstances or unforeseen roadblocks. But I wrote this chapter to encourage you to get your fighting spirit back! Become unstoppable. Go on an all-out assault. Refuse to let up your intensity for a second. Hone in on your focus and give your full effort. Make succeeding your driving passion. Impress yourself with your ingenuity, resourcefulness and tenacity. Press past your stopping points. Your stubborn persistence and commitment to your goals sends a positive message to others that no matter what, you will not be deterred. Adopt an attitude like George Allen, who said, "Health, happiness and success depend upon the fighting spirit of each person. The big thing is not what happens to us in life—but what we do about what happens to us." You have to want your goal badly enough to let go of excuses and overcome all obstacles. You become unstoppable by simply continuing to move forward no matter what *seems* to get in your way—including yourself.

Pay no attention to what the critics say. A statue has never been erected in honor of a critic.
–Jean Sibelius

## Conquer the Critics

Whenever you're on the warpath and you're making progress toward your goals, there will inevitably be haters and critics who can't stand to see you succeed. Critics never like anyone pursuing their dreams. Your effort to succeed spotlights their stagnation. Rather than using your success as a source of inspiration, critics and haters position themselves as adversaries. Their arsenal is well-stocked in the form of tit-for-tat tactics, trying to pull you back into an emotional battle. You might call them with great news that you just purchased a new car. On the outside they appear happy, but brewing beneath the surface, their guns are loaded and smoking with sarcasm. "How nice, but I would have purchased that car in blue," they retort. They're the ones who battle by playing "keeping up with the Jones'," competing with you behind your back and have a hard time celebrating your success. Their usual weapon of choice is words. They are armed and loaded with negative gossip, critical comments, snobbish statements and competitive conversations. If you haven't encountered people like this, count yourself fortunate but learn these lessons well, because you will.

Remember this: critics and haters are spectators in life and not participators. The way to win in spite of them is to elevate your own performance. Get out of the battle and go to war! You can either fall under their pressure or perform to the best of your abilities. Stop seeking the approval of your critics and refuse to let them set your agenda. When you let critics set your pace, you wind up living reactive; instead do something decisive. Use their criticism as a launch point to go on the offensive.

> A critic is someone who never actually goes to the battle, yet who afterwards comes out shooting the wounded.
> -Tyne Dally

Zero in on your goal and don't get distracted with subtle skirmishes. Go to war and fight back with achievement. Let your accomplishments remind them that they are not even in the same arena as you. No one can deny results! Your success serves as a warning to critics that you will stop at nothing less than total victory. So talk if they must; soon all they will have left to talk about is your achievements. Either way, you win!

KNOW WHEN IT'S TIME TO GET
OUT OF THE BATTLE ...

# Inspiration & Application:

- Going to war means deciding to make an all-out effort to achieve your God-given goals in spite of opposition.

- Draft a declaration of war in whatever area you need victory. Writing down your intentions strengthens your resolve and defines your commitment to succeed despite resistance.

- Count up the cost to achieve your goal. Write down five things you will have to do, buy, become or invest in order to reach your goal.

- Develop a fighting spirit. You have to want your goal badly enough to let go of excuses and overcome all obstacles.

- The way to win in spite of critics is to elevate your own performance. No one can deny results!

## CHAPTER 11

# DREAM BIG AND WORK TOWARD SOME IMPOSSIBILITIES

**"Sometimes, I have believed as many as
six impossible things before breakfast."
-Lewis Carroll**

Impossible is just a word. Most people think their dreams are impossible. However, if everyone thought that, there would be no inventions, no innovations and no breakthroughs in human accomplishment. What was once impossible is now a daily reality. Your impossible dreams are an opportunity and a gift. They pull your ingenuity, resourcefulness, tenacity and courage to the surface. They push you outside your comfort zone. You'll be amazed at what you can achieve if you really want it bad enough. Then the impossible becomes possible. If you limit yourself with self-doubt, you will never be able to achieve your dreams.

Howard Schultz is a man who dreamed big. While traveling in Italy, he saw how espresso bars were community-gathering places for friends and family. Awed by the sheer number of coffee bars in such a small country and the energy and vibrancy each bar exuded, he brought the idea back with him in hopes of recreating the Italian coffee-bar culture in the United States. Although his partners thought his idea was farfetched, Schultz stuck with it, determined to make his dream a reality. Today, Starbucks is a worldwide brand and 10,000 stores later, he's proven it pays to dream big. As inspiring as this story is, what I think is even more inspiring is that with all his success, Schultz is *still* dreaming big. With his sights set on turning China into a coffee-crazed culture outside of its

**Dream more than others think is practical.**
-Howard Schultz

tea-drinking roots and expanding heavily into India, Russia and Eastern Europe, the dream grows. Every time I sip my grande soy green tea latte, I'm reminded to dream bigger and bolder. There's no ceiling to my dreams!

## Dream In Epic Proportions

I love dreaming big, and I've found that there's no 'one size fits all' and no single formula for success. I remember when I was very young, I dreamed of being a model and image consultant. My path was a winding road but I eventually achieved my goal and reached my dream of owning my own salon and barber shop. I kept dreaming bigger. Soon I wanted my own makeup line and makeup store. It seemed the more I dreamed, the more motivated I was to pursue them. I never considered the prospect of failure because I always believed in myself and that God would give me the wisdom I needed to succeed. Plus, I was always willing to work hard at whatever I wanted.

Although it was challenging to launch my own store, I did it and had so much fun learning about business and beauty, all while being a mom. (On a side note, you can have a family and live your dreams too.) When I married my husband, my dreams took another shift to ministry aspirations. I dreamed of beginning a new type of women's ministry—one that was fashionable and fun, contemporary and relevant for today's woman. I wanted to help women everywhere get God, get glam and get the good life! Yes, you *can* have it all. Today, I'm living my dreams, all because I made a choice to dream big. I'm a mother, mogul, co-pastor, best-selling author, itinerant big. I'm a mother, mogul, co-pastor, best-selling author, itinerant speaker, wife, entrepreneur, fashionista, television personality and a host of other dream roles. However, I wouldn't have made it here had I downsized my desires or played it practical. That's the beauty of dreaming; it doesn't have to be feasible when you start. Dream beyond your means—beyond your education, experience, knowledge and skill. Dream beyond what's safe and comfortable. Dream big and then supersize it to epic proportions! The higher you aspire, the more fire you acquire. High aspirations fuel dream motivation.

> The greater danger for most of us is not that our aim is too high and we miss it, but that it is too low and we reach it.
> -Michelangelo

A small word of caution for my starry-eyed sisters: dream big but stay grounded. Dream according to your purpose and don't fall into fantasies. Fantasies always lead to failure. You will find much more fulfillment out of life and avoid a lot of frustration if you dream big in your particular bent. I can't look at my fabulous friend who is great at cooking gourmet cuisine and creating exotic recipes that delight the most discriminating palette, and decide I want to be the next Julia Child. That's not my life's bent. Although I can whip up a feast for my family when I decide to give our chef a night off, trying to be America's next top chef would inevitably lead to failure (if not a fire). Fame and fortune are certainly your portion, but on your level. It's all relative. You might be a famous beautician known all across your city. Prosper where you are and roll out the red carpet for yourself and your guests. Bring Hollywood to your home. You can be a star right where you are. Don't pack up and move, thinking all that glitters in Tinseltown is gold. There's gold to be had in the ground under your own feet if you will put in the work and start digging. Dream where you are and be great in your bent. Repeat after me, "A girl's gotta do what a girl's *called* to do." Run your race, dream big in your lane and the sky is the limit for you!

With perspective in tow, it's time to do a little dreaming! Right now, grab your favorite journal and create a list of 50 dreams you would achieve if you knew you couldn't fail. From this day forward, decide these dreams are possible for you. Dream achievement is a matter of choice, not chance. Once you choose to be a dream achiever, you begin to become one from that moment on. You send an internal command to your subconscious mind to begin going to work to make your dreams come true.

## Dream It and Do It

Achieving your dreams takes focus. Whatever you focus on, you will attract to you. When you focus on your dream, it will become more apparent. Clarity will come—the who, what, when and how will fall into place. Light will shine upon your paths. It's not serendipity, it's God divinely orchestrating your path so the dream He's placed in your heart can come to pass.

Focus on being successful at your dream, not failing at it. Success comes to those who think about success and strive for it. You will see what you are looking for. If you look for impossibilities, that's all you'll see. If you focus on dream fulfillment, that's what you'll become more aware of—how your dream can come true. Seek and ye shall find!

When you don't know what to do next, I encourage you to follow this one principle that has never failed me: *simply do the next indicated thing!* I can remember when I first had the idea to launch my own perfume. At first it started as nothing more than a fleeting thought in my time of meditation. I instantly wrote it in my journal in the present tense as something I had already achieved, "I have my own designer perfume line." Just writing my intentions was empowering. In the days that followed, it was as if my entire focus was being shifted to making that dream come true. Ideas and inspirations came to me.

While praying over my dreams one morning, a strategy for how I could design my bottles struck me and I immediately got to work researching and investigating how to make it happen. Nowhere in the process did I know exactly A-Z how to do it all. But had I not started with one little step and followed my rule of doing "the next indicated thing," I would never have the fabulous line I have today. Sometimes living your dream is all a matter of being willing to move in that direction. My husband always says, "God helps you more on your way than when you're sitting still." What can you do right now to put one pedicured foot forward? Can you write it down? Read about it in a book? Talk with someone in the industry? Spell out your dream in your journal? Create a storyboard about it and bring your desired end to life with pictures and words? There's always something you can do, so don't look for the crystal stair to the top, just step up to the next rung on the ladder to success.

## You've Got to Work It Girl!

Impossible dreams are accomplished through hard work and a plan of action. I'm not here to fill you with pie-in-the-sky notions. If you want to be successful at your dream, it won't come without effort. You must be willing to seize your moments and do something every day to make your dreams come true. Success happens with purposeful effort. You've got to put in the work.

I saw the truth of this principle so clearly in something that just happened the other day with my 11-year-old son, Ryan. It was an ordinary day at the Pierce household and I walked into the kitchen and saw my son and his friend at the table, laughing and joking with each other. I sat down and asked them what game they were playing. Ryan, laughing, responded, "Mom, we're not playing any game, we're doing our homework." I commented that they sure looked like they were having a good time with it. My son replied, "That's because we've turned homework into a game for us. We decided that we were going to stay two weeks ahead of all the other kids in the class in homework. So when we get to hang out together, we have fun challenging each other to get ahead." You could have told me that my son had discovered a new planet and I wouldn't have been more awestruck than I was at that moment. Here my son, at 11, had made a pact with his friend that most adults four times his age wouldn't have committed to.

I took away from that conversation this simple but profound wisdom for dream fulfillment: *Work hard so you can get ahead!* Where could you be promoted if you got two weeks ahead on your job? What would your financial situation look like if you were two weeks ahead instead of two weeks behind? What image improvements could you make if you planned two weeks ahead? What success could you have if you made a pact with your gal pal to work hard and get ahead? You can succeed, but you've got to get to work! Become more active about your goals and dreams.

Be prepared to make sacrifices when necessary. Occasionally, I have to give up sleep to finish a book project I'm working on or prepare for an upcoming speaking engagement. Other times, I have to make financial investments on the front end long before I see a return. If that's what my dream requires, I do it. I sacrifice now so I can succeed in the future. What can you sacrifice a little of to be more successful? Sleep? Eating out? Snacking? TV or phone time? Splurge money? Choose one thing right now to sacrifice during the next 30 days to achieve one of your goals. Watch how you drastically accelerate your progress.

Successfully reaching your dream is up to you, but that doesn't mean you have to go it alone. Get to work building new relationships with successful others. I have a whole chapter dedicated to this principle, "Get a Network of 'Get-It' People," so I won't say much here. Your dream fulfillment hangs on those you connect yourself to. You can speed up your success by finding others who are living out your dream or working at upper echelons in your industry. Read about them, write to them and meet with them. Find out what steps they took to get there, what's required and how they did it. Use that information to chart your course of action.

Girl, get busy! There's a lot you can do, but you've got to be committed to action to make your dream a reality. Like a true coach, I'm here to cheer you on. You can do this! Join the inspired and get to work making your dreams come true.

## Fears, Foes and Other Things that Can't Stop You
### (Unless You Let Them)

Most people have tons of reasons why they never fulfilled or even attempted their dream, but the long and short of it is they simply gave up. Remember this truth: nothing can stop you unless you let it. Here are my strategies for dealing with all the people and problems that will inevitably try to derail your dreams. Keep dreaming and keep moving forward in spite of their resistance and success will meet you on the path ahead.

**Fears:**  Dream it and do it in spite of your fears. Most big dreams have associated risks, but what's worse is a life spent wondering if it was possible. Many people trade their big dreams for comfort and safety, but that doesn't have to be your story.  I'm here to encourage you to go for it! A life spent going for a dream, even if you make a few blunders along the way, is more noble and useful than a life spent doing nothing.

> **I probably hold the distinction of being one movie star who, by all laws of logic, should never have made it.  At each stage of my career, I lacked the experience.**
> -Audrey Hepburn

Don't be afraid that you don't have what it takes, either.  Occasionally, I've had that sneaky little thought lurking in the back of my brain but I immediately dismiss it with a wave of my bejeweled hand.  The truth is, no one has it all when they start.  You learn through the doing. You will not succeed every step of the way. You will suffer some setbacks and fail to meet your expectations at times.  That is part of the price of admission that everyone pays in pursuing their dreams.  Conquering your fears develops your confidence and causes you to hold onto your dreams that much harder.  If you plan, work and strive toward your dreams, you will attain them.  You *can* do this, so girl, go for it!  Dream on!

**Foes:**  Overcome every opposition.  It's a sad fact of life, some people hate to see your success. Foes think that when you succeed, it's somehow at their expense.  In reality, there is a place in the sun for everyone willing to step out of the shade.  Don't disqualify yourself from your dream by listening to the doubters.  Just because they've abandoned their dream because of fear or laziness, doesn't mean you have to let them rain on your purpose parade. Learn to ignore them. Refuse to keep company with dream killers. Their toxic words will cause you to downsize your dream or magnify the obstacles.

> **Never having been able to succeed in the world, they took revenge by speaking ill of it.**
> -Voltaire

Don't succumb to those who tell you it can't be done. It absolutely can be done! I'm doing today many things my critics said were impossible or unrealistic. My imagination is my only reality. If I can dream it, I can do it. To keep my dreams fresh and fueled, I surround myself with purpose partners who share my passions, cheerlead me along the way and will happily celebrate my successes. Take a minute to assess your surroundings. Are you allowing toxic people to breed bad air? Who do you need to eliminate from your inner circle? Who are the passion partners you need to pull closer?

**Frustrations:** Fulfilling your dream is a process. Inevitably on the road, you will have points of frustration. Most people, however, can't see through the chaos of life to get to real success. People will try to distract you with meaningless drama. Life will happen and try to steer you into chaos. Dismiss the frustrations of life so you can get into real success. When you get focused, you can get through the smoke screen of impossibilities.

On days when it's tough and I have deals, deadlines and decisions up to my ears, I remind myself to stick with it. Tough times don't last always, but the persistence, tenacity and courage I develop during these times will last forever. It's in the process of making your dreams come true that you will find the most fulfillment. The pursuit is the reward, not merely the results.

Keep moving, growing and making it happen. Make adjustments, revise your dream and better yourself along the way. Whatever you do...never stop. It's when thick becomes thin that you have the greatest chance to win! So keep dreaming!

### DREAM BIG AND WORK TOWARD SOME IMPOSSIBILITIES

# Inspiration & Application:

- **Dream big and then supersize it to epic proportions! The higher you aspire, the more fire you acquire.**

- **Dream according to your purpose and don't fall into fantasies. Fantasies always lead to failure.**

- **Dream achievement is a matter of choice, not chance. You must work hard and develop a plan of action.**

- **Your dream fulfillment hangs on those you connect yourself to.**

- **Dream it and do it in spite of your fears. Most big dreams have associated risks, but what's worse is a life spent wondering if it was possible.**

## CHAPTER 12

# WHAT I LOVE ABOUT ME

**"Self-esteem isn't everything; it's just that there's nothing without it."**
**-Gloria Steinem**

"I love me!" It's a simple statement with profound impact. In a world of self-hatred, self-doubt and fear, loving yourself is one of the most innovative and refreshing things you can do to progress on your journey to success. Lucille Ball once said, "Love yourself first and everything else falls into line. You really have to love yourself to get anything done in this world." I couldn't agree with her more.

I have learned to love myself; therefore, I do not feel limited, burdened or held back by a poor self image. The quality of our lives is directly connected to our self-esteem. Often we downsize our lives to what we think about ourselves. If you have a lowly opinion about what you can do, have and be, your life's outcome will reflect that perception.

We should all love ourselves, because God does. If He loves us unconditionally, then who are we to object? Of course we all must make changes and improvements, but in this journey of life, self-love will take you farther than what anyone else can say or do for you.

The only person who can change your outlook about you is *you*.

How do you learn to love yourself? The very same way you learn to love other people. Think of things you've done that you are proud of. See your flaws without becoming a slave to them. Stop bashing yourself—be kind to your mind and love yourself unconditionally.

Try these few easy keys to loving a better you and boosting your self-esteem:

## 1. Celebrate Yourself

Your life is a party and you are the guest of honor! Celebrate every moment with love, laughter and learning. Celebrate who you are and who you are in the process of becoming. I have the courage to say, "I love me" despite my flaws, mistakes and shortcomings. My future is full and I have no time to dwell in the past.

## 2. Dress to Impress

Instead of letting your feelings dictate how you dress, dress the way you *want* to feel. It's a known fact that wearing bright colors can put you in a cheerful mood. Also, when you are looking your best, you will feel your best! You don't need a special occasion to dress up...do it for you! You deserve to look your best every day. Go ahead girl, dress to impress. It's an instant pick-me-up and the positive feedback from others will boost your confidence.

## 3. Turn Rejection into Opportunity

Every time one door closes, another one will soon open. Seize the opportunity to improve your shortcomings by making adjustments, working harder and gaining more information. Knowledge is key! Did you miss out on that last job due to a lack of skills? Increase them. Do something today

> I think all great innovations are built on rejections.
> -Louis Ferdinand Celine

to improve. The more you invest in yourself, the more confident you will be. You'll become stronger, wiser and more sure of yourself the next time your opportunity arrives.

## 4. Take Stock of Your Greatness

Get a new journal and label it *What I Love About Me.* Think about what you were like as a child, write down your most memorable achievements, special compliments given by others, special moments that made you feel great, or whatever makes you smile and feel good about yourself. Start with a list of 10 things that you love about you.

Here are a few things on my list:

- I'm always positive.

- I'm a creative thinker,  therefore I can overcome any problem.

- I think well on my feet and can make wise decisions.

- I am fashionable and style savvy.

- I stay current on my look and life.

I believe the things you love about yourself are clues to your purpose and very strong hints to what you should really be doing. All the things I love about myself have led me to the life I treasure each day.  I tracked my traits to see how they directed my life's course. Here's what I discovered:

I've always been a social butterfly.  In grade school, I was constantly in trouble for talking and socializing. Now, I talk for a living.  I am a life coach, television personality, motivational speaker and conference host.

I've been an avid reader since I learned how to read. As a child, my father and I took weekly trips to the bookstore. My thirst for knowledge is insatiable. I love to hunt and gather information; it makes me well-rounded and ready for all situations. It is also the source of my creativity.

I'm an idea magnet. I use every day as an opportunity to be creative. I walk through life with my eyes wide open, looking and listening for new ways to improve. God has blessed us all with the ability to think our way to higher heights. Through prayer and meditation, I have learned to harness my creativity to produce new products, ideas, plans and life-changing solutions.

Optimism is second nature to me. Maintaining a positive outlook helps me keep the right perspective. I insist on being optimistic because what you meditate on is what you will attract. Life has too much to offer for me to focus on the negative. This attitude has helped me overcome seemingly insurmountable obstacles and teach others how to do the same.

Fashion is my forte. I love to do everything with an air of flair. Whether it's planning a party or decorating my home, my study of style has caused me to create a fashionable life that has become my signature. Fashion is about more than just clothing and accessories. It is a mirror that reveals our attitudes, expressions and appreciations. As I run my day and help others along the way, I keep the rules of couture in mind.

Now it's time for you to discover your winning traits. My Self-Discovery Test will help you unlock your purpose and inspire you to pursue your passions. Use your *What I Love About Me* journal to record the answers to the following questions. Take some time to think about your answers—but not too much time. Over thinking will cause you to sabotage the exercise. Be honest and real with yourself; the clues your life reveal will unlock your passions and set you on the road to success.

## Self-Discovery Test

1. Describe what you always wanted to be when you were a child. _____

_____

_____

2. What do you love so much; you'd do it for free? Make a list of at least 10 hobbies that make you excited and get your juices going.

_____        _____

_____        _____

_____        _____

_____        _____

_____        _____

3. What are your special skills and talents? Name what you are known for doing very well._____

_____

_____

_____

_____

_____

4. Whose company do you most like to keep? What can you talk about for hours with that person?

_____

_____

5. Name six words that others use to describe you.

_____

_____

6. Who do you feel most passionate about helping? (i.e. women, kids, the elderly, financially challenged)_____

_____

7. What types of subjects do you like to read about?

_____

_____

8. What areas are you an expert or want to become an expert in?_____

_____

_____

9. Describe your dream workday._____

_____

_____

_____

10. Usually what you are passionate about is a problem you can solve for others. What problem do you feel passionate about solving? Who will pay you to solve this problem?

_____

_____

_____

*When you love you and know what you can do, the possibilities are endless. You can...*

**1. Promote your passions, practice and prosper.** What you love about you is what others love about you because that's what you will promote. Uplift your outlook. Become your own PR firm and share with others your positive side. Pour on the self-love so you can promote the things you are passionate about. A healthy love for self will allow you to express your skills and abilities without being afraid of failure or worried about what others think.

When you discover your passion, commit to practicing it daily. Remember, due diligence and hard work are the passage to higher earning. The one thing that all successful people have in common is an

> **Effort only fully releases its reward after a person refuses to quit.**
> -Napoleon Hill

outstandingly uncommon work ethic. The fact is, the wealthy work hard. Are you working hard on what's in your heart? Major money only shows up after massive amounts of effort have been spent.

**2. Properly love and care for your mate.** I love and respect myself and therefore I am able to be a better wife. I put a lot of time and effort into my relationship with my husband. I am careful to always look good for him, keep our home beautiful and add excitement to our relationship. Because I love me, there are standards that I just won't go below and my husband is thrilled!

**3. Prepare and impart into your children.** Whatever you feel about yourself, you will pass on to your children. When you search to find your own substantial qualities, you will be more equipped to help your children discover their capabilities. Don't

**Nothing you do for children is ever wasted.**
-Garrison Keillor

weaken your children with your lowly state of mind. Empower them to be their best. Teach them to seek out their strengths and develop their life's purpose from a young age. One of the best things you can equip them with is a low tolerance for immorality, a high self-esteem and a solid sense of who they are. Remember, you cannot pass on what you do not possess.

For the next 30 days, focus only on what you like about yourself and improving what you dislike. Do it now, there's no time to waste. Life is happening every day. Don't wait until you lose the weight, pass the class, get a new job, change your hair, get married, etc. Make the decision to *stop* waiting and *start* recognizing your self-worth now!

### WHAT I LOVE ABOUT ME

# Inspiration & Application:

- The quality of our lives is directly connected to our self-esteem.

- Celebrate who you are and who you are in the process of becoming.

- Seize the opportunity to improve your shortcomings by making adjustments, working harder and gaining more information.

- What you love about you is what others will love about you because that's what you will promote.

- For the next 30 days, focus only on what you like about yourself and improving what you dislike.

## CHAPTER 13

# PUT THINGS IN WRITING, SO YOU CAN TRACK YOUR PROGRESS

**"The pen is the tongue of the mind."**
**-Miguel de Cervantes**

Whatever you want to achieve in life, you will experience greater success if you write down your intentions before you start. This is such a simple secret, but most miss the great impact it can have on their life's outcome. You needn't be an English professor or possess the journalistic skills of Diane Sawyer to profit from your pen. All you need is a willingness to put your thoughts and ideas in writing. I live my life by this principle and have succeeded at an incredible rate as a result.

## Think in Ink!

Writing down your dreams and goals shapes and crystallizes your vision. As you document your passions and preferences, you define and refine what is most meaningful to you. Writing is an internal dialogue you have with your truest self on paper. In it, you address contradictions and obstacles to your goal and negotiate internal resources to bring your dream to pass. Very few people think in an organized manner. Writing allows you to sift through your thoughts and emerge with ideas worth their weight in gold. In fact, writing can be the spark that sets off creative ideas and strategies where none existed before.

I can remember times when I wrote down dreams and goals I had for the year and as I spelled out the details, witty ideas came to me on how to go about fulfilling them. It was as if a light bulb went off. The more I wrote, the more clarity I gained on exactly

> **"Writing is an exploration. You start from nothing and learn as you go."**
> -E.L. Doctorow

what direction I needed to move in next. That's why writing is so powerful. You can explore your dreams on paper long before you take the first step in life and greatly increase your success ratio.

Every complex decision I need to make, I work through in my own journal. Every big idea I ever had for business, ministry or self-improvement, I explored through writing. That's why I always say my journals are worth millions of dollars. Flashes of inspiration I penned years ago have come to pass and brought great wealth and opportunity to me. I have ideas in my journals that have yet to be realized that are setting me up for a prosperous future. I never take my thoughts lightly. I always capture them on paper.

Science has proven that our brains can only consciously hold between five and nine pieces of information in short-term memory. Anything beyond that and your brain can miss important connections between things and their underlying meanings. That's why writing down your thoughts is so valuable. You actually help your brain focus on solutions and gain understanding through intentional mindfulness. Until Brain 2.0 with increased gigabytes is released, it's smart to maximize how your brain works and think in ink. Capture those witty ideas on paper!

## Write Your Life's Manifesto

Writing helps you stay on the course of purpose and destiny. If you've lost sight of your vision for life or even your goals for the year, it's time to realign yourself. Write your life's manifesto. A manifesto is "a public declaration of principles, policies, or intentions." It comes from the Latin word "manifestus" which means "clear or evident." It's your written declaration of destiny, describing where you're headed and what you're all about. You need not be heir to a throne to live a royal life and commit your life's legacy to paper. All of history's greats have written a manifesto in some form or another and as a result, manifested their dreams.

*My Life's Manifesto*

My life's manifesto is to inspire others and encourage them to reach for and obtain things they never thought possible. I am ultra family-focused. I stand by my husband and commit to raising children who are kind, successful and have high moral character. I will fight to the finish for my marriage and my children. I believe in abundance. I believe in enjoying life. I work hard and play glamorously. I succeed on every level and enjoy the fruits of diligence. If I had to sum it all up in just three words, my life's manifesto is to live "pure, purposeful and prosperous."

Now it's your turn. Let's get started. Figure out on paper what you want in life and how to get it! Write down what you want to achieve, how you will build wealth, the type of relationships you want, how you define happiness and how you will fulfill your potential. Spell out your vision for your job, marriage, family and every other area of your life. What standards define you and what legacy will you leave behind? Make your intentions evident. Your manifesto must be something not only worth reading, but worth acting on.  Stop and pen your life's manifesto right now while you're inspired.

```
┌──────────────────────────────────────────────┐
│            Your Life's Manifesto               │
│  _____  │
│  _____  │
│  _____  │
│  _____  │
│  _____  │
│  _____  │
│  _____  │
│  _____  │
│  _____  │
│  _____  │
└──────────────────────────────────────────────┘
```

I am here as your life coach to push you farther than you've ever gone and higher than you've ever dared.  Your life's manifesto is meant to be big.  It should stretch you to do more, have more, become more and want more.  Don't worry about your manifesto being perfect; we're just in the dreaming stage here.  You can always go back and write a new version.

There's no failing grade awaiting you.  In fact, if you took the time to stop right now and write your life's manifesto, give yourself an A+ and go to the head of the class!

> I must write it all out, at any cost. Writing is thinking. It is more than living, for it is being conscious of living.
> -Anne Morrow Lindbergh

Next step: turn your manifesto into a life list.  Every year, I create a list of what I want out of life for that year. I think big and remove all limitations, spelling it out in detail in my journal. I call this My Dream Life List. Because I start every year like this, I usually end up crossing off everything on my list by the year's end. Often I'm amazed at how easily some things come to me that seemed farfetched when I wrote them down. I've come to realize that your life always moves in the direction of your most dominant thoughts. When you commit your desires to paper, you attract those things to you like a magnet. Create your Dream Life List now. Dream grand dreams. Think of what you really want out of this year. Expand it to three to five years if you want. Spell it out using present tense words like "I am" and "I have." Don't be vague. Write down *exactly* what you want with as much detail as possible. The more clearly you can see it in your mind's eye, the more likely you are to achieve it. Use your list to align yourself strategically for the next phase of your life. Then go gather everything you need!

## If You Can't Measure It, You Can't Manage It

Putting your thoughts in writing commits your mind to action. When you write out your ideas, you're able to develop a logical sequence of "next steps." Break down your dreams and goals into *measurable* milestones that lead up to your big goal so you can track your progress along the way. If your goal is to read more, write down your target point of reading one book each month or break it down even further and commit to reading 20 minutes each day. That's measurable. A goal of being a good reader is not! With your goal clearly spelled out in writing, you're ready to track your results.

Keep a log of your goals and record when you reach important milestones or make new discoveries. As you see yourself reaching checkpoints along the way, you will be motivated by the changes you see occurring. When you fall short of your goals or when progress seems slow, use your journal to make adjustments to your plan and keep yourself motivated. When you track your results, you stay on course, reach your mini-milestones and experience the thrill of accomplishment, which will spur you on to greater achievement.

This is why I started my own blog—to help me track my journey, and actually reach my dream weight. My blog, found at www.mydreamweight.ws, is a full-access invitation for you to read my personal muses, memoirs and motivations to reach my dream weight. In it, I share all kinds of secret weight loss tips, natural products to try and easy pointers to accelerate your results. I even offer downloadable forms to help make reaching your dream weight and developing a healthy lifestyle a piece of cake…well, maybe more of a sugar-free, low-sodium cookie.

My blog allows me to track progress toward my goal in a public manner and keep myself accountable for results on a grand scale. I've received tons of emails and comments from subscribers all over the world who say they faithfully read my blog to stay inspired on their journey to better health. Many have expressed how fun it is to track their results online with me. Girls, together we can do this! I find it so rewarding that modern technology allows me to mentor women across the world in such an easy, written format! I don't think I would have reached my dream weight without this techie-tracking tool.

Blogs are the modern woman's journal. However, I'm certainly not one to toss out physical journals as an antiquated notion, because

I'm a lover of empty books. I scour paper stores from Paris to Pensacola to find just the right journal to express my personal style. Paper stores are wonderful places with aisle after aisle of journals, specialty papers, elegant pens and assorted accessories. Explore one and stock up on a trove of treats. Purchasing writing accessories that reflect your style makes writing more rewarding. When I find a journal I love, like the pink croc one in which I penned my notes for this book, I buy every one I can find in the store. I have stacks of lovely journals just waiting to bring my ideas to life. Journalizing is a priceless part of my life so I believe in investing in the tools that will make it a rich experience.

Whether you journalize with a notebook, heavy-bound leather journal or a blank computer screen, your place on this earth is worth recording. We have records of the inspired lives of the greatest minds and world influencers in the pages of their personal journals. Most people don't know they are making history while they are doing it, but now we can see how history unfolded by reading their journals. Capture your wit and wisdom in blank books. Here are just a few secrets of mine.

## Journal Jotting Tips

■ **Make it your own**. Don't feel you have to be perfect in your journal, just put the thought on the page. Leave the "school stuff" like grammar and spelling for later or never. If you can understand the thought or expression, it's good enough!

■ **Make time for writing.** In the novel *A Moveable Feast*, Ernest Hemingway describes so well the comfortable feeling of being lost in thought amidst the hustle and bustle of the cafés in Paris that he frequented. You should never be too busy to share a quiet moment with yourself and your journal. Your journal entries do not need to be long.

■ **Make it fun**. This is your special place and your special time. Feel free to doodle, draw silly pictures or even use colored ink when writing. The more pleasurable you make it, the more often you will do it.

## Muse It or Lose It

Capture ideas on paper as soon as they come to you. Pay attention to sudden insights, ideas and jolts of inspiration that come to you and capture them as soon as you can. That's wisdom trying to speak. Some of the greatest works of art, science and music are in existence today because great men like Mozart, Einstein and Edison took care to write down their ideas. They understood that ideas were fleeting and apt to be lost if not recorded.

Often I will get many of my greatest ideas during the night season. Your dreams will reveal answers that lead to your success. I make it a

> Often an idea would occur to me which seemed to have force. . . . I never let one of those ideas escape me, but wrote it on a scrap of paper and put it in a drawer. In that way, I saved my best thoughts on the subject, and, you know, such things often come in a kind of intuitive way more clearly than if one were to sit down and deliberately reason them out. To save the results of such mental action is true intellectual economy.
> -Abraham Lincoln

practice to ask God questions before going to sleep at night. I write out the questions and by morning the answer has come in a dream form. The other night I was looking for a product name, one that fit perfectly. I wrote in my journal the question I had for God, "What's the perfect name?" I went to sleep and voila—I had a dream. In the dream, a song was playing over and over again. When I woke up and pondered the dream, I realized the song was loaded with answers—the name of the product, the commercial concept to market it and the motivation I needed to launch the product, all wrapped up in one song. So profound! Only God's infinite wisdom could relay that message to me. Pay attention to your dreams and record the details.

The benefits of writing are available to all, but only an inspired girl on the grow will truly grasp these principles and take action. I'm confident that person is *you*! Grab your pen, pencil or keyboard and write your way to an inspired life. Who knows, maybe one day I will be reading a biography about your fabulous feats and thrilling achievements. I can't wait—make it a page-turner!

## PUT THINGS IN WRITING, SO YOU CAN TRACK YOUR PROGRESS

# Inspiration & Application:

- When you commit your desires to paper, you attract those things to you like a magnet.

- When you document your passions and preferences, you define and refine what is most meaningful to you.

- Write your life's manifesto. You need not be heir to a throne to live a royal life and commit your life's legacy to paper.

- Set measurable goals so you can manage your progress. Keep a log of when you reach important milestones or make new discoveries.

- Ask God questions and record your dreams. Answers are often revealed in them.

## CHAPTER 14

# EVERYBODY LOVES TO SHOP!

**"People spend money when and where they feel good."**
**-Walt Disney**

Everybody loves to shop! Shopping is a wonderful exchange to express who we are and what we love. We all love spending our available funds on things that mean something to us. However, what you may not know is that shopping is an art, a system that can be used as a tool to help catapult our success to higher heights. You may not be a mall maven, but there is a lifetime's worth of motivation and insight that comes with retail done right.

## Shopping Speaks of Me

My devotion to shopping is not just limited to my fancy for fashion. I enjoy the hunt for finds that enhance every area of my life. I may pursue my purchasing passions at the bookstore, searching for new and interesting information and resources. You could find me at the toy store, buying new games and learning tools that I can use with my son. Maybe the search is for new and edgy designer clothes for my daughter. Or, I might find an interesting collectible to add that je ne sais quoi to my home. Of course, I love to pamper my husband, coordinating ties and shirts, cufflinks and accessories for his suits. Sometimes I am in pursuit of tools that I can give to my staff to help them work more efficiently and pump up their productivity. Finding interesting gifts that I can send to my friends is one of my favorite pastimes. I shop for what speaks of me and to me. My purchases reflect what I think is important in life and how I want to share in the passions of those around me. Most of my shopping is actually for other people, although I cull my share of the couture. Shopping is the thrill of the hunt, the joy of the catch and the fun of hauling your loot home. Every hunter knows the best trophy is the target that almost got away.

## Everybody Loves a Purchase for Their Passion

We all like to shop for the hobbies that have our hearts. Admit that you enjoy the freedom to put your money where it matters to you most. If you love your children, you probably spend a large portion of your income on their appearance, their pursuits or their activities.

Sports enthusiasts love to shop. Golfers invest in tees, balls, gloves and every imaginable form of club cover. Don't even get me started on bowlers. Is there an end to the possible combination of shoes, bowling balls and bags that can be purchased? For the bona fide technophile; also known as a "techie," with ever-expanding technology, there is something new for them to shop for every week. If you consider yourself a gourmand, you like shopping for the newest restaurant to visit.

As a young girl, my father took me to seminars and conferences that hosted some of the world's best motivational speakers and businessmen. He gives credence to the Cynthia Nelms' quote: "If men liked shopping, they'd call it research." My father would never admit it, but he likes to shop too, though information and idea starters are his preference. He pursued his passion for knowledge just as fervently as any woman at a half-off shoe sale, often with me in tow. No matter your predilection, the options are endless and we enthusiasts seem to keep trying to conquer the beast we love.

**The quickest way to know a woman is to go shopping with her.**
-Marcelene Cox

Shopping with someone is an accurate look into their heart and mind. Shopping is self-reflecting and revealing at the same time. It is easy to see my passions and purpose if you shop with me. You would find out I am inquisitive and curious. I like to see the newest and latest of anything, whether clothing, books or music. I love information, because we would definitely make an extended stop at the bookstore. I am generous because I would find something to take home to others, whether my friends or family. What you are willing or not willing to spend your money on, says a lot about you. Will you only shop when on sale, never paying full price? Does that mean that you are on a budget or that you only consider yourself when it is discounted?

## Shop and Smell the Roses

Let's pause for a moment and recognize the beauty that shopping really brings. Every shopping adventure helps you to see the possibility for more and better. It is difficult to be gloomy when shopping, because the array of possibilities is invigorating. Shopping shows there is always more than enough to go around. What a happy sight to pull into a car lot and see multiple rows of cars available. One day you may choose from the lot. Learn to look at shopping as a visual mind multiplier. There is a reason it is called retail therapy. If taken as an art, shopping can be beneficial.

Everybody loves being motivated and shopping is a motivator. Seeing and desiring what's available can be an influential motivator for work. Even the proverbial American dream—a house, a car and two children requires shopping—at least for the house and car.

Only people with an attitude tightened by poverty shun the fun of shopping. Never allow your current economic situation to shape an inaccurate belief system. When you can't afford to buy, go window-shopping and use it as a catalyst for increasing your productivity to increase your income. Don't condemn those who through hard work and discipline are now enjoying the fruit of their labor. You can change your situation. Be careful not to allow yourself to get mad because you *aren't* able to shop; or get envious of others who are. Desiring things is natural. Right your financial life so you can enjoy what is ultimately one of the most pleasurable of life's experiences.

Friends don't let friends shop irresponsibly, so with a few insider tips, you'll be both smart and savvy. You can shop like a rich girl on a real girl's budget by following these simple shopping dos and don'ts.

## Shopping Dos

- Do shop high and low. You can buy luxe for less if you have a keen eye for a good buy.

- Do shop to keep yourself and your family well-dressed and stylish. Identify which stores fit your family's lifestyle and frequent them.

- Do shop for inspiration and ideas for your life's call.

- Do shop for bulk buys. When you're good at finding a bargain, you can live a higher quality life at a lower cost. When you find shoes you love, buy them in multiple colors. When your favorite jeans go on sale, buy more than one pair. Bulk buys save time and money later.

- Do shop for experience. Expand your vision by handling

goods on the next level. Test drive your dream car. Try on designer shoes equal to one month's paycheck. Sample until you can spend.

## Shopping Don'ts

■ Don't spend money you don't have.

■ Don't spend frivolously and buy things you don't need. Practice discipline. If it doesn't fit, match or work, leave it or return it. Waste not, want not.

■ Don't buy something solely to keep up with someone else.

■ Don't shop to satisfy negative emotions. What's worse than a bad day is a bill you have to live with for months to come.

■ Don't spend money that you should be giving away to church or charities.

■ Don't become a renegade for retail and allow shopping habits to ruin your reputation or relationships.

Shop within your means, purchase meaningful things and you will sleep very peacefully at night in regards to your buys. If you are shopping just to prove a point, keep up with others or put on airs that you are someone you're not, then my dear, you're on the verge of shopping till you flop. Shopping is a fun way to enjoy, educate and enhance yourself, not a means to try to equalize yourself with those you may envy. Shop smart. Your trips to the mall, market or marts should make life better, not add mayhem.

Everybody loves gaining helpful information and shopping is about being inquisitive. Learning to see is a talent. You can gain a wonderful education just by visiting high-end stores and observing. I really wanted an understanding of why some clothes are more expensive than others. I set myself to get educated before I could ever afford the clothes. I would visit boutiques, talk to salespeople and try on items. It does not cost to dream. You can learn your likes and dislikes. Discover which designers mesh with your personal style and which do not. Touch the finest before you ever purchase it. I did. I inquired without shame and I built relationships with salespeople who now have me on speed dial. I was not intimidated, and my dream eventually became my reality.

Early in our marriage, we would plan small shopping trips. Each year we would save to go to a big city of our choice. At first we could only afford to stay a day or two. We would go with our modest budget and have a good time learning and exploring. The more we traveled, the more acquainted we became with the city and the more we were able to do. Each year we would up the ante, either by upgrading our hotel, going to bigger and better stores or staying a few days longer. Today, our shopping trips are more than annual and we do it first class. We stay in five-star hotels, we have a limousine driver who meets us and we shop all the fashion hot spots. But we did not start out that way. We started with a passion that we cultivated little by little until our desire motivated us to produce better so we could experience better.

> **Buying is a profound pleasure.**
> -Simone de Beauvoir

We used our shopping excursions to increase our exposure, which ultimately increased our lives.

Whether lavish or simple, educational or indulgent, whether you are saving, sowing into others or splurging on yourself, in one way or another I believe everybody loves the art of shopping. So come on, it's OK.  In fact, it's fun.   Everybody loves inspired living and shopping can help you acquire a habit and master an art that can accompany you in life all the way to the top.

EVERYBODY LOVES TO SHOP!

# Inspiration & Application:

■ **Purchase purposefully.  Shop for what speaks to you and what speaks of you.**

■ **Shop savvy and save.  You can live a higher quality of life for less.**

■ **Shop and gain knowledge and insight on higher-level products and lifestyles.**

■ **If you aren't able to shop, don't get angry, get active and produce more.**

■ **Be willing to admit that you enjoy the freedom to put your money where it matters to you most.**

## CHAPTER 15

# CREATIVITY IS YOUR KEY TO INCREASE

**"Creativity can solve almost any problem. The creative act, the defeat of habit by originality overcomes everything."**
**-George Lois**

"The war of creativity never ends!" So said my son Ryan who, at the time of discovering this profound truth, was only ten years old. In fact, his pinch of creative insight has produced his own company. While sitting in one of the concluding sessions at my Women's Success Conference, Ryan began to sketch a crest depicting what the creative process means to him. Across the top of his sketch-pad he scribed, " The war of creativity never ends" and thus, the logo for his new Boy Brilliance company was born. The Boy Brilliance line consists of clothing and accessories for boys with a bright future, available at **www.boybrilliance.com.** Teen boys everywhere love the fashionably fit look "head of the class hoodies, "smart t-shirts" and "cool thinking caps" while parents love the positive, school-affirming messages behind the clothes. To date, Boy Brilliance is one of my son's most well-received and lucrative business ventures. His love for creative activity has led to his increase and inspired people, young and old to stay in the fight for creativity.

You *do* have to fight to stay creative! Amidst the hustle and bustle and never-ending race of the world, you must strive to tap into your creative edge. Don't let a passive, lackluster attitude capture your creativity and hold hostage the dream life that you desire to live. You must press to make a daily effort to release your God-given creative abilities.

Why the battle? Anything of high value or that can bring increase takes a fight to obtain or gather. Creativity is not only valuable, it is necessary—not just to sculpt a famous sculpture like The David or paint the ceiling of the Sistine Chapel, but to increase your finances and your lifestyle. Make no mistake about it; everybody needs creativity. You may not need the creative genius necessary to construct the pyramids of Egypt, but you just may need the creativity that keeps the kids clothed and fed in lean financial times. Or you may find the need for the creativity that keeps a marriage alive in a world of separation. You might find it useful to have the kind of creativity that keeps young people focused on morality in our society of deteriorating moral standards. As a CEO, creativity is needed to scout out new talent and keep increasing your bottom line. Surely, the creativity that finds a way that you *can* do it when the whole world says you can't will definitely come in handy on your road to success. Believe me my darling, *everybody* needs creativity. It's just a matter of what, when, where and how.

## Creativity Defined

*Webster's Dictionary* defines creativity as: "the ability to transcend traditional ideas, rules, patterns, relationships, or the like, and to create meaningful new ideas, forms, methods, interpretations, etc.; originality; progressiveness; imagination." I define your creativity as your God-given intellect coupled with artistic intuition to produce or birth something new.

Creativity always provides a new beginning. It's your way out of your present situation. When you are facing a challenge, you aren't supposed to quit; you're supposed to get creative. When you're in need of financial increase, you aren't supposed to cower down to your circumstances; rather, you are supposed to get creative.

> There is a fountain of youth: It is your mind, your talents, and the creativity you bring in your life and the lives of people you love.
> –Sophia Loren

Creativity manifests itself in a variety of ways. It can be artistic, scientific, enterprising or most uncommonly noted, practical. The sad thing is that so many people have convinced themselves they have no creative ability. That is simply untrue. God created every one of us with the ability to be creative; our creativity just has to be developed.

Why is creativity the key to increase? Because executing outstanding ideas is what makes money in today's world. Creative people are the ones who dream up the ideas that become new products or a better way of doing something. Creativity is at the core of innovation, invention and increase. You have that creative ability inside of you!

## The Creative Approach

**Be creative daily.** Your life needs your creative input. Ask God for creative ways to make your day more productive. Each morning, I wake up happy and focused. I ask God to direct my path and give me creative ideas to make the most of my day—and He does. Every day is a gift. Time is the most precious commodity we have. Once it's used, it can't ever be regained. So be serious about how you spend your 24 hours. If you are not being as innovative as you should be, it's time to take action. Assess what's hindering your creativity. Do something about it immediately!

Make immediate changes for immediate manifestation. For example, a picture is worth a thousand words! Carry your camer and begin to take photos of everything that inspires you. Start doing something creative right now; you don't have a minute to waste!

**Be creative where you are**. Sometimes we fall prey to the myth that we must relocate to activate our creative ability. You don't have to uproot yourself to become more creative. You don't have to jump from job to job or be flighty in your business ventures to be creative. There is no magical location or ideal position where creativity abounds. Learn to be creative where you are. True creativity can produce ideas for the job you have right now.

Be creative and productive enough to prosper right where you are. Stay-at-home mom Anna Ginsberg got creative right from her kitchen and made a million-dollar meal. Ginsberg always had a passion for cooking and creating meals her family and friends enjoyed. One day, she decided to put her innovative ideas and cooking ingredients to work for her. Working from home, Anna started creating recipes that began to make her rich. In 2006 she was the grand prize winner for the Pillsbury Bake-Off, winning $1 million cash and $10,000 in kitchen appliances. In addition, she has made multiple television appearances on shows such as Oprah, and The Today Show. Anna has also won nearly $20,000 in other cooking contests. How can you get creative right where you are? It's time to stir things up and get cooking with your creative thinking!

**Be creative with what you already have to work with.** If it takes a big budget for you to come up with an idea, you have the wrong concept of creativity. Real creativity works with what's available. Creativity is about making something out of nothing and working hard to make it grow. Start with what you have to work with. You don't need the grace to finish until you get started. To help you get going, here are some ways I sharpen my creative edge.

## Practice Creative Calm

Chaos is not conducive for creative thought. Sometimes we have to rest and relax to become productive and profitable again. This is not license for laziness to take root. Rather, it is wisdom for the workaholic. You must find time and a place for solitude and serenity. Find a clean, quiet spot to sit and think. God's creative power does not work well when subjected to clutter and confusion. Protect your quiet time and quiet place because it's precious. There are times when your mind calls for stimulation to get your creative juices flowing. Yet more often than not, creativity needs a quiet place to cultivate.

My luxurious bathroom is my place to peacefully ponder. The other day while showering, subtle ideas began to come to me. At the time, I was strategizing over how to come up with $10,000 in two weeks for a project. Then, Voila! An idea came to me out of nowhere: "it's in your house!" I got out of the shower and began to look around my home. I saw an item I was thinking of selling. Without hesitation I put the item on sale that day. Two days later, it was sold and I was a total of $10,000 richer! There is a passage of scripture that tells us that if you tune in diligently to the voice of God, ideas, answers and strategies to set you in a higher place will come to you. Find your quiet place of peace where you can tune in and hear ideas from on high.

Is your environment stifling you? Do you and your family have the house in disarray? Declare a family work day. Go on a cleaning and cleansing binge. Clean the clutter: bring a new freshness to your life.  Inspiration will flow in an inspiring environment! Your opportunity awaits you!

# Get a Focus on Fashion

I'm often inspired by the couture collections that rule the runway each season.  Fashion is both fluid and steady.  I love fashion.  It's always fresh, enlightening and new.  The world of fashion is a consistent source of inspiration, because creative expression is at the core of its existence.  Every time I see the color, cuts and coordinates revealed on the runways, I'm motivated to create (and shop for) something new!  Fashion stirs me to add class and flair to my projects, to be bright and bold in my attitude and project glamour into all the areas of life where it seems the thrill is gone.  Become more fashion-focused and like me, you will be compelled to add more style to all you do.

# Ask Questions

Staring at the problem harder will not cause a sudden strike of inspiration.  We must ask the right questions to jar us into new jurisdictions of creative thought.  Creative minds continually ask questions.  The proper questions will trigger your curiosity toward a more creative flow.  Whenever I'm working on a project, I ask the questions that lead to a successful outcome.  Asking negative questions like, "Why can't I get this? What's wrong with me?" will give you answers that lead in the wrong direction.  Pose your inquiries with positivity. Ask, "What do I already know that is helpful?" "Where have I successfully solved similar problems?" Your mind will flow in the direction in which you pose your questions.

**You see things;**
**and you say "Why?"**
**But I dream things**
**that never were;**
**and I say "Why not?"**
**- George Bernard Shaw**

I also make a practice of asking God questions. Whenever I am at a point of decision in my life, I usually inquire of God right before I lay my head down to sleep. His creative nature always comes to my rescue, speaking to my innermost parts, subtly whispering my answers. Listen within; the creative solutions you need are waiting.

## Cultivate an Innovative Environment

Here are my three Bs to bring more creativity into your breathing space:

**1. Break your routine.** Add something new to your schedule. Take a different route to work. Strike up a conversation with someone outside of your circle. Try new cuisine. Walk instead of drive. Try a new hairstyle. Get to work earlier—anything to just change things up, and creative thought is sure to show up.

**2. Brainstorm.** Gather the most stimulating people you know and sit down for a sharing session. Conversations with other creative minds always spark ideas. Assign a person to manage the flow of thought so you stay on target. Aim for a lot of ideas. Then make rules such as "no question is stupid" and "don't judge" to regulate the air of the meeting. Keep things loose because a stiff, sterile environment isn't likely to encourage creative play. Write everything down in order to make the most of the genius you've gathered. Afterward, be sure to evaluate your session to make it even more effective in the future.

**3. Be outrageous.** Begin to have fun again. Creativity often strikes in the midst of happy thoughts and good times. I've had many ideas while having a wonderful time with friends and family.

Do something off the wall and expect to experience the wonder of innovation.

## Discover the Wonder of Working

Get to work, my friend. Creative genius is never sparked by lazy habits. Ideas come through concentrated, hard work. To be good at what you do, work hard. Creative ideas often come after you've worked hard and gained knowledge of the process. Work hard and be a finisher. The creativity that produces profit doesn't just stop at generating the ideas or concept; it finishes the job by applying that idea and producing the end result.

**Work brings inspiration.**
-Igor Stravinsky

Wherever it's used, creativity is a vital tool for success in life. Average people lack ideas. You have to be innovative to get ahead in life. Creativity is about divine inspiration, thinking the impossible and doing what others haven't done or won't do. Throughout my life, my creative ideas and daring nature have given way to wonderful endeavors that have been both profitable and impactful. Key in to your creative abilities and increase your life in more ways than you can imagine!

## CREATIVITY IS YOUR KEY
### TO INCREASE

# Inspiration & Application:

- Creativity is your God-given intellect coupled with artistic intuition to produce or birth something new.

- Be creative where you are, with what you already have on hand.

- Find a quiet place for creativity to cultivate.

- Ask questions for innovative answers. The proper questions will trigger your curiosity toward a more creative flow.

- Ideas come through concentrated hard work.

## CHAPTER 16

# SAY THANK YOU

**"In our daily lives, we must see that it is not happiness that makes us grateful, but the gratefulness that makes us happy."**
**-Albert Clarke**

In your quest for success, you must always remember to say thank you. It's not just an etiquette nicety; it's an essential part to living a successful life. Saying thank you is really a simple task that is underrated and underutilized. Somewhere between when mothers gave their daughters their first set of of stationary and the email age, we've lost the art of giving thanks properly.

At some point in life, someone will help you meet the right person, get to the right place or invite you to the right event. Acknowledging others' help along the way, is not only good business, it's good manners. No one owes you anything and no one is required to help you, so when you receive the smallest of courtesies, it is simply appropriate to acknowledge it with a thank you.

## Grateful Girls Get Ahead

When life grants you connections in high places, be thankful for the opportunity and exposure. Gaining access to an exclusive network or being introduced by someone with great influence can launch your career into higher heights. Give credit where it's due. I know what it's like to have someone open the door for me and to open the doors for another. Gratitude is in order. Here's a priceless piece of wisdom that I learned early on in life: always acknowledge and appreciate whenever someone uses their influence, power or authority for you.

Say thank you quickly and lavishly. I spend a lot of time and money saying thank you. I never allow someone to help me in any way, large or small, without acknowledgment. Whether I am thanking my employees, consumers, friends, family or mentors, I am always careful to recognize them and show appreciation.

This is how I keep excelling in life—by saying thank you and remaining grateful. My husband and I have received life-changing advice from our mentors that saved us much money and years of trial-and-error methods. Our mentors have exposed us to new levels, shaped our thinking and encouraged us to be and do more. Through it all we remain thankful in our heart *and actions*. We know talk is cheap so we show appreciation by sowing financial gifts into our mentors, advisors and VIP relationships. This shows them that we are grateful and deeply value their time and wisdom.

When favor is flowing your way, having a grateful heart will not only get you in the door, it gets you invited to the table. People are more likely to pull you close when they feel they can trust you and know that you appreciate their efforts. You can literally change your entire life and get to where you're going a lot faster by simply seizing the opportunity and maintaining an attitude of gratitude. Walking in the footsteps of another person's success always makes the way easier.

Appreciate the favor that flows your way, but don't stop up the

stream with bad mentee manners. Listen intently when in the
presence of mentors and apply their counsel immediately. Never
compare yourself to them or overstep your boundaries in the

> **Pride slays thanksgiving, but an humble mind is the soil out of which thanks naturally grow. A proud man is seldom a grateful man, for he never thinks he gets as much as he deserves.**
> -Henry Ward Beecher

relationship. Girls on the rise, be
wise. Mentors and advisors are
precious commodities. Treat them
as such and you'll never have to
regret learning the value of a
relationship once it's lost.

Once you get a leg up, be sure to
reach a hand back. Pass favor and mentorship to those under you
as a token of appreciation for the favor you were afforded. Say
thank you by making a difference in another's life. It's the cycle
of success in operation here girls!

Don't assume thanks are limited to earth-shattering feats of generosity.
When you are committed to express appreciation, you will notice
the small acts of kindness that envelop you daily: a note to a child's
teacher for investing in their future, a note to a friend for listening
when you needed a sounding board or a note to a co-worker for
taking extra time to show you a new program. If you really try,
you can say thank you a lot, and you should. Develop the right
thankful attitude, because gratitude never goes out of style.

## Good 'Ol Fashioned Gratitude

The real secret to saying thank you is having a grateful heart.
Gratitude is an outward expression of an inward heart condition.
What's in your heart? Are you truly grateful and content or secretly
feeling like you were owed better? Here's a quick self-test. When
you didn't get that perfect gift in just the right color, how did you

react? Did you display a fake smile and a give a weak "thanks" or were you grateful that someone thought enough to celebrate you at all? Of course, we say "thank you," but being grateful takes it a step farther. It causes you to reflect on the favor and connect with the giver in a special way.

Gratitude and thankfulness show good old-fashioned humility. It goes beyond a thank you note or an expected reply. It's part of a bigger picture, a philosophy that you must adopt for continued success in life. We really should give thanks in all situations. Maybe you didn't have a perfect day, but at least you woke up to experience it. You may not love your current job, but you should thank God that you have one! Some money is always better than none! You may be overcoming a sickness, but thank God that you are healed and still alive to appreciate life.

> Develop an attitude of gratitude, and give thanks for everything that happens to you, knowing that every step forward is a step toward achieving something bigger and better than your current situation.
> - Brian Tracey

## Gratitude Does the Body Good

I have a friend who was diagnosed with cancer and given a negative report. The doctors immediately began with chemotherapy. I gave her some of my books and my son Ryan's book *If You Think You Can You Can, If You Think You Can't You Can't* to keep her spirits lifted. Throughout her fight with the disease she remained positive and always maintained an attitude of gratitude.

When she had to leave her job for months to be treated, she told me she was thankful they allowed her to take a leave of absence. When she lost her hair, she was thankful that she found a few stylish wigs to wear. She was thankful for the materials I gave her because they strengthened her faith. She was thankful for her physicians, thankful for her family and most of all thankful to God for giving her the strength to fight back. Even in the face of death, my dear friend remained thankful to God and to others. Even when bedridden, she never allowed herself to become bitter or ungrateful with her circumstances.

Today, my friend has a clean bill of health. There is no sign of the cancer, her hair has grown back and she just got promoted on her job. Not to mention she is more thankful than ever! I believe she overcame this challenge due to her grateful and positive attitude.

Your health is connected to your attitude of gratitude. Studies show that individuals who face terminal illnesses with a positive attitude have a better chance of living longer, and tend to be more resilient and successful in life. Being grateful will help you maintain a positive outlook and remain in faith when you need it most. When you learn to appreciate what matters, you can stay motivated that your current situation can and will get better soon.

Take a pause for the cause. Right now, write down all the things you are thankful for. Try to come up with at least 25 things. Remember to include the big and small things. Your list may include people who have helped you, things you possess, experiences you were afforded, places you've gone or simple everyday things that are easily taken for granted. Once completed, this exercise will bring you tremendous perspective, peace and power as you realign your life with a more grateful approach.

**If you learn to appreciate more of what you already have, you'll find yourself having more to appreciate.**
-Michael Angier

# Stacia's Secrets for Saying Thanks with Style and Grace

Having a heart of gratitude is only as good as the habits used to express it. Here are a few of my stylish suggestions for saying thank you with fashion and flair.

■ **Put it in writing.** It is always nice to give an immediate verbal response to a kind gesture, however, it's even better to follow it up with a written note of thanks. I'm not talking about scribbling out a quick "thanks for the ride, you're the greatest!" No, take time and acknowledge the deed and tell a friend, coworker, boss or mentor how much you appreciate what they have done for you. Make a mark by writing something meaningful. Every occasion calls for appropriateness. While a handwritten note is often most valued (due to its vintage quality and scarceness in our day) there are still other ways to give a meaningful thanks. My friends and I often send text messages with quick notes of kindness, sometimes just to say, "thanks for being my girl, you're always there for me." Now, of course this is certainly not our *only* form of communication. Text messaging is our informal way to show our gratitude and by no means a substitute for sending a proper thank-you note when necessary.

■ **Be grateful with a gift.** Send a thoughtful thank-you gift to someone who went out of their way for you. Do research if you must to ensure the gift is something they will like and will find useful. When in doubt, cash is always convenient.

Not long ago I was greeting people from the audience after a speaking engagement. A lovely, stately looking woman walked up to me and pleasantly greeted me. Along with her strong accent, her sincerity rang clear in her voice. "I really enjoyed your presentation," she said. "You are such an encourager! You may not remember," she continued on, "But one year ago I came to talk to you. My child and I were homeless. I explained my situation and you gave me wisdom to change my situation. You told me that I didn't have to stay that way and could go from victim to victor and live well. You took it one step further and told me that I could change my life in one year if I really wanted to. Then you gave me instructions.

"Today is one year from that day! I followed your instructions and example and now I've gone from being homeless to making thousands of dollars each week. *You were right, I didn't have to stay that way.* I wanted to let you know how much I appreciate what you did for me and as a token of my appreciation, I have a gift for you." With that she handed me a blank check and told me to fill in any amount I wanted. I wouldn't fill it in and told her to just give whatever she felt in her heart. Her gift was a sizeable amount, which was quite humbling. I was deeply touched not only by her success story, commitment to change and blind obedience to good instruction, but also by her gratitude and gift. She didn't have to come back and say thanks, but she did.

Sometimes your situation can cause you to adopt a victim mentality and think someone owes you, but this woman's story is proof that the first step to being a victor in life is to follow the counsel of those willing to help and appreciate the hand that helped you. Thankfulness leads to total and complete restoration
.

■ **Collect stationery to share your sentiments.** If you have the tools to write a quick thank you note, you are more likely to write it. We have an assortment of thank you notes in our home. Some are from the entire family and each family member has their own personalized stationery. I also collect fun and fashionable note cards that express my personality. Preparing yourself to say thank you makes for a more pleasurable experience when the opportunity arises to show your appreciation.

■   **Pass on the praise.** Right now, make a list of all the people you need to thank and why. You are more likely to perpetuate good deeds and favor by taking the time to say thank you—and meaning it! Everyone likes to be appreciated, and if people feel that you actually notice the nice things they do for you, they are more likely to give an encore performance.

■   **Act on your appreciation.** A note of thanks via email to your staff is sure to boost morale. Phone an unsuspecting friend to share your appreciation. An unexpected verbal message is always warmly received. Take action during the next 24 hours. Write a note, make a call or send a gift. Do something to express your gratitude and appreciation today!

SAY THANK YOU

# Inspiration & Application:

- It's not just an etiquette nicety; it's an essential part to living a successful life.

- The real secret to saying thank you is having a grateful heart.

- Your health is connected to your attitude of gratitude.

- It is always advantageous to send a written note of thanks for any kindness or favor shown you.

- Express your thanks with a gift when appropriate.

## CHAPTER 17

# FIGHT FOR YOUR LOVE AND MONEY

**"Are you gonna wait for a sign, your miracle? Stand up and fight."**
**-Kenny Loggins**

Are you ready to rumble? This boxing battle cry has transcended the ring and has rung clear through countless competitions. Today I pose the question to you. The fact that you are reading this book indicates you want to live an inspiring and successful life. However, to live an exceptional life takes effort; in fact, it takes fight. I'm sure you have noticed a number of combative analogies throughout this book. That's because love, money and good living aren't bestowed upon the passive. Rather, they are awarded to those willing to stand up and fight for the best life possible. Let's start by being honest, with all pretenses aside. Everybody wants real love and everybody wants money. Anything in great demand will require a great defense to maintain. If you don't fight for love and money, you won't keep either.

## You Can't Win If You Won't Get in the Ring

Be courageous enough to get in there and demand and defend the good life that is your divine right. You can have an amazing marriage, raise outstanding children and gain wealth beyond your wildest dreams if you just step up. Don't forfeit your rights to a good life just because you are afraid to get in the ring. Stop backing down to bad times, bills or any other of life's blows that may come your way. It's easy to stand by and watch others become champions while you sit ring-side and complain about societal ills. Yes, the divorce rate has skyrocketed, raising quality kids has become quite a challenge and poverty has permeated our nation. Negative news and circumstances will always anguish the average. However, you don't have to be a statistic. Champions face their opponents and envision victory.

## ROUND ONE: Fight For Your Love

Marriage is a sacred vow before God between a man and a woman to commit their lives to one another. It's at the core of human relations and is vehemently defended by God. Today, when people see a solid marriage, it is all at once encouraging, enviable and almost unbelievable. Thankfully, it is not unattainable. You can have an amazing marriage. You just have to focus and fight to do what's right.

A great marriage is your choice. There are no shortcuts to a fulfilling marriage, but you can get started down the path by taking responsibility for your own actions and attitude. Be committed to improvement. Become the person you wanted to marry. A good marriage begins with you. As your life coach, I'm going to share with you *what works* for loving your man, increasing your intimacy and becoming lifelong friends. If you're ready for the training camp of champs, read on.

**Fight to Stay Together and Stay in Agreement.** In this world, you simply have to make a conscious decision to stay with your spouse. My husband and I made the decision from day one that we were going to stay together and stay in agreement no matter what. I'm my husband's biggest fan and he is mine. I support and help wherever I can. He supports and encourages me to stretch farther and reach higher. We pray and stay congruent with one another's goals. Even when we have a difference of opinion, we agree to keep the peace and our agreement causes us to prosper.

Sit down with your mate tonight and talk about the state of your agreement. Make a list of ways that you can be supportive of one another. Then make a promise to each other to stay together forever!

**Fight to Get the Right Information.** We face negative influences each day that could keep our relationships on the run, but don't be bullied by bad information. Fight for the news that will nourish your nuptials. My husband and I host a marriage retreat every year and hundreds of married couples attend from all over the region. We always tell couples that attend that they need to hear the information over and over again. After the retreat, they are amazed at the results of listening to the tapes and implementing what they heard. News about the retreat has spread to the friends and family of those who attended and many couples are ordering these audio messages (**www.lifechangerscc.org**) and experiencing the same marriage-improving results. Getting the right information will rev up the romance in your marriage.

**Fight to Say the Right Things.** We never use the words "divorce", "separation", or any related phrases in our conversations or disagreements. Words are powerful—they bring life or death to a situation. I understand the power of words, so I use them to my advantage. Daily I declare that we will stay together forever. Every day I say good things about my marriage and my mate. It's easy to get into the societal swing of sour speech. But fight the powers that be and keep your speech about your relationship sweet. This week, practice saying loving and encouraging words to your spouse first thing in the morning and right before bed. Watch what a difference your words will make!

**Fight to Spend Time & Stay Friends**. Protect your relationship. Most successful marriages are ignited by love, but sustained through friendship. My husband and I are friends *and* lovers. An enormous part of our enduring love is that we really enjoy each other's company. Our schedules are incredibly busy and it would be very easy for us to go weeks without going on a date. Yet no matter what, we carve out time weekly to spend with each other. Our companionship cements our relationship, keeping it safe and solid. Become each other's best friend and have fun together. This week, plan a date with your mate to refresh your friendship.

> A successful marriage requires falling in love many times, always with the same person.
> -Mignon McLaughlin

**Fight to Keep Your Marriage Passionate.** My husband has never become immune to the charms of the chase. And I enjoy being caught again and again. We flirt with each other often and keep our touches tender. Don't allow your love to chill. Small actions each day can ensure the passion never fades. Look into each other's eyes when you chat. Communication is intimacy. Every spouse desires to be touched, held and appreciated. Tender actions throughout the day ignite the anticipation for passionate play later.

**Fight for What Fits**. My husband is a very powerful man. He is an incredible leader and wonderful father. As his wife, I am the link to the legacy he wants to create for his family. I am able to help with his business affairs as well as have the spiritual insight to assist him with his vision. I make sure that I have the image and panache that make him proud. I dress up for my husband and he assures me that I am his "good thing." I was made for him and he treats me like that every day.

There are always other choices, options and offers, but we fit perfectly. My husband has created an incredible life for our family. Not long ago, I told my husband that if I had to do it all over again, I would say yes to him again! I can't replace him in my life because we just fit; and he and I have made a choice to fight for each other. Fight for what fits. A good marriage is much easier to work on than it is to replace. Do something out of the ordinary for your mate today to affirm that they are the most important person in your life.

Along with my marriage, my relationship with my children is both remarkable and irreplaceable. Every single day, my husband and I have purposed to train, impart and surround them with incredible amounts of love and security.

## ROUND TWO: Fight For Your Children

**Fight to Prepare and Impart into Your Children.** Believe in your children and train them to succeed. Expect them to be exceptional and encourage them to do the impossible. Educate them on doing what's right. It takes no effort to pass by your kids every day without really communicating with them. Often, we are more informed about our favorite television show than we are about the lives of our children. You must defy the norm and fight to lay a foundation on which your children can build their future. My husband and I have poured years into preparing our children for the life that lies ahead of them and we couldn't be more proud.

While preparing for a presentation I asked one of my assistants, "What are some things that you know about me that most people do not?" She is around me almost daily so I was very interested to hear what she had to say. "I see your interaction with your children and what they learn from you. There is not a day that goes by that there isn't a conversation or instructions about finances and life lessons."

Her keen observation was true. My husband and I never allow a day to pass without teaching our children something they need to know. We're preparing our kids to leave our house filled with wisdom to build wealth! We teach them daily about saving, sowing and money responsibilities. We have also committed to instilling the habits that will make them happy, healthy human beings of high caliber.

Whether it's a direct one-on-one lesson or learning from observation, our children are being imparted into with life-shaping lessons every time we are together. The same is true for your children. The question is, what are they learning while around you?

Fight to prepare and impart into your children. Build the relationship by talking with your children daily. Get to know them. Show them love and share your wisdom. The life that you demonstrate to them is the life they will duplicate.

## ROUND THREE:  Fight for Your Money

**Win The War Within for Wealth.**  No one gets rich by accident. Even an inheritance takes diligence to claim. You won't ever experience prosperity until you admit you want to be wealthy and understand that's what God wants for you. The war for wealth begins within. Pretending you don't care or displaying a "take it or leave it" attitude will leave you defeated on the path to abundant living.

Maybe some of you are saying "I don't care about money; I don't really want any. Money isn't an issue." I profusely disagree. Money *is* an issue! If you do not want money, you do not want the things it enables you to do, like providing comfortable, safe housing for you and your family. Or, providing better education options for your children. Money allows you to travel and see and create experiences that make life rich. Money affects the kind of food you eat and the places you go. Your level of wealth determines how you can tend to your health and even how you and your loved ones leave this earth. Money is an issue in nearly every area of your life. It takes hard work, wit and war to obtain. So more likely, it's not that you don't want money, you've just given up on what it takes to get it.

God intended for each one of us to live a rich, fulfilling life without the pain of living paycheck to paycheck. However, we must catch up to God's intention. If you are in need of increase and your finances are far from where they should be, take note of these keys to combat that will ultimately help you increase your cash flow.

**Fight to Better Your Financial State.** You may not have had any control over how you started in life, but it is certainly your choice what financial state you continue in. Your financial future is created by you. So assess where you are and get a vision for abundant living. Make a "prosperity

> Whatever may be said in praise of poverty, the fact remains that it is not possible to live a really complete or successful life unless one is rich.
> -Wallace D. Wattles

board"! Go to the store and purchase a few money and lifestyle magazines and a tri-fold display board. Clip and cut pictures, words and phrases depicting what abundance looks like to you. Paste images of you and your family prospering on the board. Look at your prosperity board every single morning and visualize yourself living out the pictures. Make some external changes that are more congruent with your internal vision! Over time, your financial state will rise to meet the pictures imprinted on your imagination.

One way to use visualization to build your faith for more is to write yourself a check for the amount of increase you want to see over a year's time. Post it up where you can see it often and believe for that amount of increase to come in. I've tried this and it works. Your imagination is a God-given tool to help you create your reality. Fight to picture better and you will perform and prosper on that level.

**Fight for Your Financial Plan**. Gather all the information you need to create a battle plan to prosper. Create a written budget. Find out how much you owe. Plan out every purchase. I plan everything and check everything. I check my bank accounts daily. I keep my money organized in my purse. I respect the resources that I have, keep order and expect overflow. Every day, a million things are fighting to get your money. Make a plan and fight to stick to your blueprint for better.

**Fight to Ask for What You Want.** We've all heard people mention the old cliché, that the world consists of the "Haves" and the "Have Nots." I believe that the world consists of the "Asks" and "Ask Nots." I am a firm believer that you have not because you ask not. A significant part of getting what you want out of life and situations is simply not being afraid to ask. Champion your cause.

Recently a young woman fresh in the field of banking came to me with some serious concerns about her career. Her department was doing the worst in the region and needed to raise its performance significantly to stay afloat. With her job in jeopardy, she had come up with a plethora of plans, strategies and action steps, then came to ask my advice. After hearing the entire ordeal, I simply replied, "Have you asked God how you can do your job better?" She smiled and admitted she hadn't, but would that night. A few weeks later, she returned with an even bigger smile. God had given her a great idea and she implemented it immediately. Her idea caused the area to rise from the bottom to take the lead. Her superiors had been so impressed with her performance, they promoted her to run her own branch. She went from sinking to soaring in her career and all she had to do was ask.

I have negotiated incredible terms, received exclusive information that should have been out of my reach and increased my bottom line, all because I was not

> **If there is something to gain and nothing to lose by asking, by all means ask!**
> -W. Clement Stone

afraid to ask. Fight the fear and ask for what you want, and you too can perform great financial feats. Right now, identify what it is you really want: A better marriage? A promotion? More wisdom? A better price? A particular contract? Take time to write a list of what you want, then get quiet and go ask for these things.

**Fight to Save.** Building wealth is a battle. Most Americans have overspent and accumulated a significant debt load. Many appear to be prosperous when in reality they are living paycheck to paycheck, just a few days away from financial disaster. Don't let that be you. Learn to save your money. This week, open a new savings account, even if you just start with $25. Your money cannot grow if it has nowhere to go.

**Fight to Sow.** We are a family of true givers. Not only do we give 10% of our income to our church, we give to special projects and programs. We make a practice of giving good gifts and helping others whenever it's within our means to do

We make a living by what we get. We make a life by what we give.
-Sir Winston Churchill

so. We fight to sow because that is the foundation of our financial health. I believe that giving creates a cycle of generosity for your life. Learning to let go and be liberal is the most important link to long-term wealth. Most successful people including John D. Rockefeller, Andrew Carnegie and Joseph Colgate acknowledge that the secret to their incredible fortune was that they regularly gave away 10% of their income. I believe that if you want to live big you have to give big! This week, give something away. Become a consistent tither by sowing at least 10% into your local church and you will begin to experience a life of abundance and increase.

**Fight to Spend Wisely**. Don't spend money just because you have it. Never be frivolous or emotional with your finances. Know why and where you are spending. Learn to make a few high-end purchases and mix them with low. This will keep your life looking luxurious for less.

**Fight for Financially Friendly Relationships.** My closest friends and associates are all very prosperous, therefore, our conversations are full of wisdom and ideas as we swap wealth-building strategies. Consider those closest to you. Do you spend your time talking about not having enough or ideas to have more than enough? Refuse to discuss and debate money matters with people who are not prosperous. Get a dream team of people around you who want to increase. Remember, those who surround and support you will shape your mentality and determine your ability to increase.

**Fight to Take Action.** There is a lifetime of information packed into this chapter. Don't wait another minute. Don't give yourself another excuse. Just take one thing and do it today. They may seem like simple steps, but the habit of putting principles into practice can make you unbeatable.

The higher life is yours if you're willing to put up a fight. You're the champion of your life and your mate, money and children are counting on you to be the winning woman you are. Grab your gloves and go for it girl!

FIGHT FOR YOUR
LOVE AND MONEY

# Inspiration & Application:

■ **Fight for
divine right.**

■ **Fight to get the right information and keep the
right relationships in your**

■ **Fight to stay in agreement with your**

■ **Fight to prepare your**

■ **Fight to take responsibility for**

## CHAPTER 18

# LEARN TO TRAVEL
# WITH YOUR EYES OPEN

**"We live in a wonderful world that is full of
beauty, charm and adventure. There is no end to the adventures
we can have if only we seek them with our eyes open."**
**-Jawaharal Nehru**

It is very easy to live on autopilot day in and day out—doing the same tasks, on the same path, seeing the same people, places and things. It is no wonder the new and fresh ideas that are needed to live an inspired life seem to elude us. Whenever good ideas seem rare, it is time to breathe new air. The best way to escape the mundane is to break out through travel. Learn to become a modern-day explorer. What are you looking for? Inspiration, of course!

John Galliano, one of my favorite designers, once said, "I love to travel; it's what inspires me. Creativity has no nationality, so I don't want to leave a stone unturned." As a fellow globe-trotter, I understand how he can derive so much inspiration for his couture fashion designs from his traveling exploits. I acquire so much inspiration when I travel. I find that the uncommon and unfamiliar can be invigorating.

Travel allows you to live (if only for a few days) in an ideal world. Everything about traveling helps to pull us away from the daily distractions that prohibit us from being able to slow down, observe and imagine. Great ideas rarely grow in the vacuum of mundane living, but they flourish when we stretch outside our norm and envision new possibilities. Pursue the possibilities of innovation by choosing to travel with a purpose!

> **Travel and change of place impart new vigor to the mind.**
> -Seneca

There are a host of reasons for anyone to travel, but here are a few that ring true for me:
- Travel to replenish yourself
- Travel to spend quality time with your family
- Travel to educate your kids
- Travel to escape with your mate
- Travel for research
- Travel for business
- Travel for creative ideas
- Travel for training

## Adventures Near and Far

A passport to a foreign country isn't always necessary to expand your thinking. A simple change of climate and local flavor can make a huge difference. One of my family's favorite places to travel to is Florida. We all enjoy the warmer climate immensely. As soon as we hit the tarmac and the jet hatch is opened, the balminess of the breeze alters our perspective. Just shedding that layer of coats lightens us physically and mentally. We feel different as we trade gloves and hats for sandals, tank tops and sunglasses. I gain more colorful and inventive ideas as I walk the streets, the flora and fauna coloring the path. The new pace of any location can trigger you in subtle ways. When I visit Manhattan, it is frantic and fast-paced. It feels like everyone is moving quickly and accomplishing business, so most of my entrepreneurial inspiration is sparked in this East Coast hub. In Florida, an inventive motivation emerges as I feel less encumbered surrounded by a more relaxed lifestyle.

It's a big world out there. Expanding your mind through travel and life experiences will fortify your faith to do big things. When you have a world view, you are less likely to be hindered by a little local opposition to your life's goals. Go global, girls!

## Wisdom from the Well-Traveled

Although I haven't quite made it to the four corners of the earth, I've certainly seen a few splendid sights and been on my fair share of exciting adventures. While off on my jaunts, it's rare that I travel to escape. Rather, I travel to engage. I want to learn more about the world, other foods, people, places and life itself. I determine to absorb every last detail when I travel. It's sad to see people who talk about vacation as "getting away from it all." I travel to glean and to grasp insight, ideas and inspiration to bring home and "get back to it all." Go on vacation, but refuse to mentally vacate. Ideas abound for a globe-trotting girl with a keen eye and an active, inspired mind.

I find hotels to be a source of prolific ideas. Plush hotels pay consultants millions of dollars to decorate and furnish their rooms to help guests feel relaxed. Hotels are usually the first on the forefront for the newest innovations in decor, such as high-end mattresses, high thread count sheets and bathroom accommodations. I observe all of the details we enjoy on the road and take them home with me. I incorporate them into our home atmosphere and in our church's hospitality departments. Other hotel guests may appreciate the niceties, but I appreciate them enough to record and use them for inspiration at home.

My husband had the idea of having "courtesy clerks" at our church after visiting a top-of-the-line hotel offering this service. He wanted to bring that superior service experience home to our congregation and guests.   We researched their uniforms and trained the department to duplicate what we encountered in that grand hotel. Today, all of our guests are able to freely receive a little taste of posh pampering by implementing a travel-inspired idea.

> **Travel is more than the seeing of sights; it is a change that goes on, deep and permanent, in the ideas of living.**
> -Miriam Beard

## Travel with Two Sets of Eyes

To capture inspiration on the road, you must arrive armed and ready to seize the moment.  Always have a camera on hand to photograph your fascinations. Take snapshots of window dressings, storefronts, display cases, store or hotel décor and anything else that sparks ideas for your life's ambitions.  So many times I have discovered a new idea for my business while walking down the streets of big cities. I take a quick snapshot and now I have a visual cue that I can bring back as a reference for my staff to help me execute.

## Travel for Leisure and Learning

Many of my protégés use travel not just for leisure, but for learning. One couple discovered a quaint idea during their honeymoon travels.  They found a boutique hotel in Miami for their stay.  Boutique hotels are small, but luxurious.  The bathroom was tiny, but she noticed the shower rod was not the usual straight one, but rounded out.  She noted what a difference it made: the small shower seemed out. She noted what a difference it made: the small shower seemed larger because the bowed rod caused the shower curtain to be farther away. Upon returning home, the couple surfed the web and found the "crescent" shower curtain. One phone call later and it was delivered to their door. Voila! They brought the chic sensation of a boutique hotel into their bathroom at home.

## Lists for Those with Wanderlust

**Make a Travel To-Do List.** You will make the most of your trip by operating according to an agenda. I don't travel anywhere without an agenda. This allows me to soak in as much of the destination as possible.

**Make a Travel To-Gain List.** Take mental inventory. What do you want to gain from this trip? What is the "return home" value of your travels? Will you return home with a better understanding, appreciation and love for your spouse? Will you have a closer relationship with your kids? Will you have more insight to complete a project? Will you be inspired to write a song, or paint a masterpiece?

**Make a Travel To-Learn List.** What would you like to learn on this journey to a new location? Designate your desired goals to gain knowledge and learn something new. Always be on the lookout for information to educate yourself about your purpose and the world around you. A well-traveled individual loves to learn at each destination.

## Travel Like the Best, for Less

Don't worry, you won't be left behind by reason of your budget. You can always travel well for less. My husband and I consider ourselves pretty savvy travellers. We travel several times a month for business as well as pleasure. Our accomodations are usually luxury resorts and hotels and we enjoy fine dining and stylish transportation. I love traveling in high style. While I do love a luxe lifestyle, I also appreciate a discount tag. Why pay full price when you can get a deal? Although we comparison shopped and got the best rates we could find, it still seemed like there had to be a way we could get a better bottom line.

Then one day my husband and I learned a secret from wealthy friends of ours who had an insider's edge. You can travel for less— much less—by becoming your own travel agent. Travel agents get discounts and deals that far surpass any offer to a general consumer. By being an industry insider, you can enjoy tons of perks including room upgrades, first-class flights at coach rates and even free trips to exotic locations! It saves you money and makes you money. As a globetrotting girl, I simply couldn't let this deal pass. "Sign me up," I said, and that was the beginning of a new travel company for my husband and I. By becoming our own travel agents, we can travel for a fraction of the cost and enjoy major discounts on airfare, hotel accommodations, rental cars and even dining worldwide. It's the perfect avenue to save money while fulfilling our travel desires. Now I'm here to pass this secret on to you. Become your own travel agent, too. It's about simple dollars and sense! Visit **www.lifechangerstravel.com** for full details. See the world and save!

Start where you are and keep moving forward. If you can only take a day trip and drive to a new location a couple hours away, go have a grand time!  Just be sure to look and learn so that you upgrade your life.  Then, budget to stay longer next time.

However you travel, wherever you travel and whatever your reason for traveling, do so with wide eyes of expectation.  It always results in new and interesting discoveries.  Whether you are globe trotting or going just around the bend, plan an adventure to inspire you!

---

### LEARN TO TRAVEL WITH YOUR EYES OPEN

## Inspiration & Application:

- **Whenever good ideas seem rare, it is time to travel and breathe new air.**

- **Expanding your mind through travel and life experiences will fortify your faith to do big things.**

- **Always have a camera on hand to photograph your fascinations.**

- **Travel for leisure as well as learning.**

- **Become your own travel agent and see the world at a fraction of the cost.**

## CHAPTER 19

# GET A NETWORK OF "GET IT" PEOPLE

**"Surround yourself with only people who are going to lift you higher."**
**-Oprah Winfrey**

The secret of a good life is to surround yourself with the right people. Who you know will determine how high you go. If you realized the value of your network to your net worth, you would be more particular of whom you choose to befriend. Some people consider their grocery list with more scrutiny than they give their friendships and associations. If you are going to live an inspired life, you must become more discerning about who you surround yourself with.

Build a network of "get-it" people. These are people who understand who you are, where you're going and what life should be like. Your dreams are nurtured by chatting with those who are in the know. Such talks can birth new dreams inside you, motivate you to do more and encourage you not to quit. Stay away from intimate relationships with people who don't get your dreams, your work or your life. Their careless and clueless attitudes will steer you off course.

Who are you allowing to accompany you on your life's journey? Are they coaches or critics? Assess their lives. Do you want to become like them? Do you want the results they are getting? If the answer is no, then it's time to choose a new inner circle. I did this and turned my life around!

## My Three-Year Turnaround

Years ago, my husband and I had a treasure trove of people who we thought were friends, buddies and conversationalists. As I evaluated my life, I realized my relationships were not impacting my life plan in a positive way. There are actually people who do not complain about money problems, who love and admire their spouses and who are proud of their kids. My observation was that none of those people were talking to me. What you allow to surround you will infiltrate you like a bad odor. You can't live in a stinky house and walk out smelling fresh, and you can't fill up on nonproductive conversations and leave producing achievement and success.

We made a decision to move with the movers—who were moving up, that is. We went on a journey to change our network and to prove that who you hang around determines where you will hang out. You can squawk and complain with chickens, or soar with the eagles. I was sick of being in the hen house; I wanted to breathe rare air. In three short years, we got rid of the people who were wannabes and met people who really were genuine. We kicked out the discouragers and the people who questioned why we wanted a better life. We started meeting people who lived the good life and our lives changed for the better. We changed where we vacationed, who our children interacted with and where we shopped. It was uncomfortable at first, but discomfort eventually led to profit. We actually began to see a better bottom line in every area of our lives. We went from barely getting by to having more than enough. Why did all of this happen? Because we changed our associations.

The new relationships changed my perspective and helped me to see better methods for living a good life. I increased my financial portfolio when

> **Friendship makes prosperity more brilliant, and lightens adversity by dividing and sharing it.**
> -Cicero

I discussed finances with people who had experienced greater financial success. The people I shopped with changed my wardrobe and the experiences helped me to tweak my image in a new direction for the new doors of opportunity that came my way. We learned and earned a new way of life by changing our conversations. Penny ante dialogues were traded for million-dollar discussions that offered us solutions. If we experienced a challenge, we had people who could offer instruction and advice, and not just compare their bad situation to ours.

## Network and Learn From the Bottom Up

If you want your income to increase, hang with people who have money. You can't let the higher life intimidate you or you will avoid those with wealth. Appreciate when those living the good life pull you close and expose you to better. Exposure creates desire. Celebrate when someone lifts the shades of mediocrity in your mindset and lets you look in on the good life. You might not have it yourself at first and may have to start as only an observer. If you hang around it enough, eventually it will rub off on you.

One of my favorite movies is *Sabrina*. Near the end of the movie, Thomas, the chauffeur for the Larabee family, confesses he is really a millionaire. He explains that while he was driving around Mr. Larabee, he learned what Mr. Larabee invested in and how he operated financially. Thomas imitated what he saw his boss do and prospered. That's wisdom! You can hate on your help or learn from them. I think celebration and imitation are much more profitable.

My daughter's personal assistant and her husband have learned this lesson well. They have become personal and travel assistants to our family and as a result, where they eat, how they shop, what they drive and where they vacation have been upgraded. Everything

**Celebrate what you want to see more of.**
-Thomas Peters

went up through association! They are living the million-dollar life without actually having the funds. If you're willing to learn from successful others in your life, you too can profit.

## In the Know or Out of the Flow?

Your relationships can keep you in the know or out of the flow. Choose friends who actually know what will help you advance in life. If you are not satisfied with the quality of your life, you need to cast a scrutinizing eye over your advisory circle. They are probably in the same economic, career and relationship state that you want to be freed from. The best way to increase your net worth is to increase your network. It is widely acknowledged that your income is the average of your five closest friends. Your shared manner of life makes you similar peas in a pod. Your activities, patterns and conversations are typically all the same. I can predict where you will be in five years by the books you read, the places you go and the people you hang around. If your friends don't read, don't travel and don't have relationships with movers and shakers, neither will you.

## Raise Your Relationship Standards

Build relationships like you would construct a house of cards— very carefully. Allow yourself distance to see if each new friendship is really worthwhile. Your choice of friends does reflect your values, so pay attention. What is the nature of your relationship and conversations? Do they center on complaining or encouragement?

What will your friend allow you to get away with? Friends should be a checkpoint for your conduct. A true friend should never allow you to get away with anything that is detrimental to you. A true friend tells you the truth, regardless of your reaction or opposition, because real friends care more for your well-being than for your emotions. Scrutinize your judgment—do you choose friends because they are just like you or because they are good for you? Remember this: you don't need a lot of friends, just a few good ones. Choose wisely.

> **The antidote for fifty enemies is one friend.**
> -Aristotle

## Detox!

No, I'm not recommending you grab your girls and head off to a desert hot springs spa to cleanse your mind and body (although that would be fun); I'm talking about detoxing your relationships. Purging your relationships is to your spirit what a Swedish massage is to your body. It will rejuvenate you and bring you greater calm. When was the last time you evaluated your relationships and the impact they were having on your health, wealth and well-being?

A great friendship takes effort and aplomb, but should never be a liability. Don't waste your words with problematic people who treat you poorly. Take this quick association assessment: Out of a group of friendly, nice women, do you always find the jerk in the crowd—the obnoxious one, the gossiping one or the broke one? You attract what you are. Pessimistic people are drawn to pessimistic people. Fix what's going on in you and you will attract better. Make it your practice to hang around the best, not just the accessible. It may cost something (usually an attitude adjustment and a little self-improvement), but these relationships are priceless. If you hang with bottom feeders, you will be at the bottom. Don't get left behind; who you hang around will keep you in the know! Stop now and write a list of all of your most important relationships. Honestly evaluate how they are affecting your life. How do you feel when you leave the presence of the people who surround you? Who do you need to draw closer to and who do you need to pull away from? Ask God to give you wisdom on what friendships to maximize and which ones to minimize or release.

I have great girlfriends in my life. My friends and I are very girly together, not catty. We don't spend time gossiping about others or backbiting each other. We truly enjoy spending time together and doing fun, girly things like shopping, spa moments and vacationing. It took some time to find friends who really understood my lifestyle and purpose. My relationships were sifted and shifted in certain seasons. C'est la vie! Everyone you start out with will not be everyone you finish with. Sometimes you change, they change or the situation that brought you together changes. But there will be those lifelong friends who are called to stand beside you and who genuinely celebrate you and want to see you succeed (and vice-versa). These are your divine purpose partners. We all are meant to have these relationships in life. Go on a crusade to connect creatively with those you feel validate you and your purpose.

## Beware of Double Agents

Weed out double agents in your network. A double agent is the friend who always has the inside scoop on people who don't like you. Years ago, I had a few of these people in my life, but one day I woke up. I realized in order for them to get their scoop, they had to play it both ways—pretend to be my enemy's friend as well as mine. Needless to say, that revelation marked the end of our association. Don't be deceived. If a person in your network is always making you think people are against you, that person is too. Get rid of the informer and her informants!

> **Whoever gossips to you will gossip about you.**
> -Spanish Proverb

## Befriend Biographies

If you are so deeply surrounded by people who don't want to progress in life or don't want you to progress, you may need to find an ally in the pages of a book. Mentorship via a library card is valid and extremely rewarding. The word 'author' is derived from the same root as the word 'authority' so you can assume the pages of a book contain the expertise to change your situation. I always say successful people leave clues, but you have to be willing to search for them diligently. They usually disclose their philosophy for success and the habits that pushed them to the top.

When my children were young, we spent every Saturday at the bookstore. We would find magazines and books about places we wanted to travel to someday. We read biographies about great achievers, explorers or inventors. No matter how tight our budget was, my husband and I always set aside money to buy books. When you want a new direction in life, you have to create a flood of new information and relationships. What three topics could you read about right now to improve yourself and get ahead in your personal or professional life? Go to your local library or the bookstore and pick up a book in this area today. Begin to read your way into a higher quality of life and relationships.

## Get Ahead by Being a Giver

Your network is only as strong as the maintenance you put into it. Value your mentors, friends and important people in your life by being an asset to the network. When you help those in your network succeed, eventually the favor will flow your way. Sometimes the favor flows from the hand you fed, but many times it comes from another. You will always reap what you sow, but not necessarily where you sow. That's why I don't hesitate to share freely of my time and resources with my friends and mentors. I constantly look for information that will help those in my network. I keep in touch with important people in my life and go to great effort to send gifts and cards to recognize special days and celebrate their successes. Many times what I do is not necessarily reciprocated because I am sowing into people who are more successful than me. I believe in sowing upward. I sow where I want to go. If you want relationships with people on the next level, then you must give on the next level. Be creative in finding ways you can be of service. When you help other people get what they want, you can get what you want.

## Networking No-Nos

The most important rule of building a fabulous network is to never try to compete with those you need favor from. Don't be in the presence of greatness so you can compete with them. Learn the process so you can duplicate it on your level, not theirs. You violate your network when you try to be something you are not. If you are welcomed into the company of people who offer you advice, counsel or just a glance into the better life, earn their confidence. Be trustworthy. Learn to sit and to be quiet, especially when you don't understand. Often a misunderstanding is a lack of knowledge. Answers to many of life's questions are learned in time, so just appreciate the opportunity to breathe rare air. Be a girl who "gets it" so you can attract a network of people who "get it."

## GET A NETWORK OF "GET IT" PEOPLE

# Inspiration & Application:

- ■ The secret of a good life is to surround yourself with the right people.

- ■ Your relationships can keep you in the know or out of the flow. Choose friends who actually know what will help you advance in life.

- ■ When you want a new direction in life, you have to create a flood of new information and relationships in that area.

- ■ If you want relationships with people on the next level, then you must give on the next level.

- ■ Never try to compete with those you need favor from.

## CHAPTER 20

# DRESS THE PART IF YOU REALLY WANT THE ROLE

**"Know first who you are; and then adorn yourself accordingly."**
**-Euripides**

Your inner brilliance cannot shine through generic packaging. So, dress it up! Become the go-to girl in your industry by dressing the part. Look like you mean business and people will take you seriously. When you step into a room, your personal appearance should say, "Hey look at me, I'm your girl, I can take you to the next level." Let your look establish you as an authority, as one people can trust and want to do business with.

You only have a split second to let everyone know what you are about. Your personal appearance is telling your story long before you open your mouth. Commit to putting your best self forward at all times. Convince others you're the best in the business by looking like it. When your goods are wrapped up in a superior presentation, people will think you're worth an investment.

## Package Yourself for Success

Consider this: each day you are presenting a visual resumé for yourself. That resumé is telling everyone whether you belong in the executive boardroom or the mailroom. Where would you rather be? To get the starring role, you must dress the part. The doors of opportunity have always been open to me, but only because my physical preparation matched my mental determination.

I stay current on the fashion trends and know what is appropriate attire at all times. Many women miss this; they strive to look so unique that they don't fit in at all. Every industry has style standards, so assess yours. Whose look on another level do you admire? Do you look like someone worth promoting? The only way your boss can see you in a more powerful position is to visualize you there.

Winners look like winners and dress to show others what kind of opportunities they are ready to embrace. Every time I started a new phase in my life, it was preceded by a change or upgrade to my image. I can remember every pivotal and monumental moment in my career and what I was wearing. Though my looks were different, I was—and still am—impeccably polished. I am committed to looking my best at all times.

You don't have to have a flawless face and a perfect body to look polished. It's about affording yourself star-quality status by paying attention to the details and optimizing what you have.

You will put forth the effort to look your best when you believe you are worth it. I'm here to tell you that you have what it takes to look your best. You have what it takes to take care of yourself. You have what it takes to practice good grooming and personal hygiene. What's the secret? A little bit of effort and some beauty basics. I call them my Beauty Bill of Rights. Yes, it takes work to look your

> When you dress professionally you feel more suited for the job. You feel the authority, the professionalism and the respect internally, and you project that out onto the world.
> -Diane Reichenberger, CEO

best, but the basics are what we all should be doing anyway. Stars get stylists to help keep their look captivating, actresses have costume designers to help them get in character and you have me, your personal style coach, to help you look the part.

The rules of fashion are timeless traditions that are suited to help any sophisticated lady. My Beauty Bill of Rights are amendments that help me define my style and maintain a fierce and fabulous look. They remind me of the standards I must uphold. Follow these tidbits and you will be a step above the rest.

## First Amendment: Thou shalt always love and care for thyself.

The first step to a refined look is to remove the phrase "low maintenance" from your vocabulary and upgrade your way of thinking. I'm not saying you must become high-maintenance, but a refined look certainly requires some maintenance. Let's face it: the 'wash and go' is not your winning look.

Be sure you have the beauty basics in place. Don't slack when it comes to personal hygiene. Take showers, brush your teeth and comb your hair every day. Create a winning routine that you can maintain daily. Don't take shortcuts. You can never be too tired to wash your face or too rushed to shower. There's nothing worse than a woman in a Missoni dress with unshaven legs or wearing Gucci sandals while in desperate need of a pedicure. Take ownership of your look. There is no need to subject yourself to a day's worth of insecurity because you took shortcuts in your daily routine. Put forth 100% effort every day. Now, repeat after me. "I will not take a day off; I will look my best every day." Always remember, when you look good, you feel good—I promise!

## Second Amendment:  Thou shalt glean from the glamorous.

If your endeavor is to upgrade your style, learn to linger a little longer around those who have the look. Who inspires your personal style?  List your style mentors, past and present.  A good place to look for a style mentor is among those who have the job or career path that you desire.  Observe the way they carry and present themselves.

I know a young lady who always had long hair.  One day she walked past with a sophisticated shorter cut.  She was working in the banking industry and noticed all of the females in higher positions had shorter hairstyles.  After much consideration, she realized that although her hair was attractive, it was portraying her as a younger, immature and less responsible new hire.  To land her banker role, she needed people to trust, respect and believe in her ability to help manage extensive portfolios.  She made a change to help her career and showed everyone that she fit in with the higher level of management.  I thought that was a great personal epiphany for a young career girl.  Do not allow your novice opinions to be detrimental to your dreams and goals. Successful women know that an evolved sense of style adds to their personal power.

> While clothes may not make the woman, they certainly have a strong effect on her self-confidence — which, I believe, does make the woman.
> -Mary Kay Ash

## Third Amendment:  Thou shalt exude high style.

Create a style for yourself that portrays a distinguished persona. It will set you apart from the crowd.  A surefire way to get noticed and remembered is by defining your style.

My personal style is glamorous sophistication.  I mix glitz and glamour with classic elegance. I love vibrant colors, rich fabrics and tailored suits adorned with exquisite baubles that clearly speak to my personal taste. I like to excite the senses with my look. I make my statement with bold accessories that captivate the eye. I leave my mark with a sweet aroma of my signature scents. My perfume Inspire embodies all that I love. It's a sensual blend of fresh fruits, orchids and a secret blend of musk to add passion and flavor. It's a sophisticated scent that can be worn day or night.

Become an extremist. Invest the best part of your budget on the items that are on your extremities—your head, hands and feet. Make sure your hair and makeup are in tune. Invest in good quality shoes, a great watch and a distinguished handbag to upgrade any outfit.

If your accessories are illustrious, the rest of your outfit will blend in, causing people to interpret your entire ensemble as slightly more elite. I developed my jewelry line for Stacia's Style Shoppe just for this purpose. When I began shopping in higher end stores, I learned that increasing the quality of my accessories elevated my entire look. I decided to make star-styled jewelry available to women trying to build their wardrobe accessories at prices that would not bust their budget. This gave many of them the extra pinch of panache they needed to upgrade their look and begin walking into doors of bigger opportunity because they looked the part.

Save up for the good stuff! It's worth it! I recently recalled the first time I bought a designer purse. I walked right into a Prada store with the cash I had saved for the purchase. I was very excited and proud about being able to buy a pink Prada bag. It was a rewarding experience because I cut a picture of that bag out of a magazine, pasted it up so I could see it often and saved up to buy it. What an experience. Saving up for that bag helped me upgrade my thinking and boost me to a new level. There's a sense of independence and opulence that comes over you when you know you have the freedom to make a big-ticket purchase.

## Fourth Amendment: Thou shalt plan thy look.

Whatever your style, determine to be at the top of your class. Of course this means you'll have to plan for it. Planning your look will help temper you from being a slave to the sales rack or falling into a trendy trap. When you know your style, you know your standards. You learn what works for you and you stick to it. Hold every garment to your standard. If it doesn't fit—don't force it. Stay true to you and preserve your fabulousness!

Every season, I plan my look. I buy all the latest fashion magazines and tear out images that exemplify my style, then I create a vision board to meditate on daily. Having the board as a constant reminder helps me when I'm getting dressed and when it's time to shop. I also make a shopping list of things to buy. The list keeps me focused when I'm in stores. Often, I'm able to get what I want at a great price because I am focused and prepared.

To create a winning style, you have to be savvy and creative. You don't need to be decked out in red carpet attire to get a call back. A little high end and a lot of low equal an effective look for any casting call. Don't break the bank to look like a million bucks.

## Fifth Amendment: Thou shalt be an A-list lady at all times.

As you dress for your dreams and pursue the role of a lifetime, you must now learn to carry yourself like a leading lady.

"A-list" status requires the ability to speak with authority. Speak calmly and deliberately. Your conversation reveals your thinking, your point of view and your knowledge base. Recognize when you are in the company of people who require you to actively listen, and not absent-mindedly talk. When you don't know, choose not to speak. Make your words count by using them sparingly. Only the most rare commodities are treasured, so make others lean in closer to listen by speaking when necessary, not excessively.

Leading ladies have a presence of strength. They are women who can stand in the spotlight because the light of scrutiny is unable to unearth any inconsistency. It is not wise to aspire to a high seat without cleaning up what can be analyzed negatively. Evaluate yourself accurately for flaws that can inhibit your success. Sure up any weak spots in your character and fix what can make you fail. Greatness requires the most work in the beginning, building a solid foundation of good nature. Primp, polish and then poise yourself for success.

Women who stay on the "A-list" earn their keep with their gravitas. They always play their role to perfection. There are no cracks in their stellar armor. They are always above the fray and live in a drama-free zone.

Nothing makes a woman seem more simple than the appearance of pettiness. "Petty" means small and if you major in small complaints, frustrations and offenses, you are destined to produce small results. Act regal if you want to be treated regal. Living life large is not always easy—everyone will face his or her share of challenges— but remembering the big picture will help you to maintain a sense of decorum in the storm. Very few things are worth what can be lost when you allow the heat of the moment to make you lose your cool.  Learning to think quickly yet respond slowly goes a long way in helping you to handle hot situations.

A-list ladies have a stellar entourage.  Surround yourself with people who lend class to your status.  If you hang around those who are cunning and petty, they will eventually make you into a cunning and petty person.  You will have the habits and ideals of the people who enter into your personal space, so guard yourself. Evaluate those you give ear to: are they the best examples of people working toward a better life, or just those that complain about the life they are living?

Inspired living is within your grasp, so dress to impress and call to attention those who matter.  Once you have the floor, work it with a regal flair.  Make every moment count and this could be your most productive and stylish year ever!

## Parting is Such Sweet Sorrow

You've made it to the end of this book, hopefully much wiser and more inspired than you started.  I told you I was here for you as your life coach, so when you need a pep talk or just a nudge to keep going, growing and dreaming, pick up this book again.  I wrote it as a reference tool for an inspired life. Pull up a chair, cozy up to your favorite chapter and we'll talk again about the good life! You're an inspiration to me and the reason I live my life as I do— so I can be a role model for you to show you that success is possible and not as far away as you think.  You have what it takes on the inside of you and now you have the knowledge you need to bring it to the surface.  So get going girl, get going!  Your success awaits! Be inspired!

DRESS THE PART IF YOU
REALLY WANT THE ROLE

## Inspiration & Application:

■ Package yourself for success by looking your best each day.

■ Love and care for yourself by putting effort into your beauty routine.

■ Glean style tips from the glamorous.

■ Invest the best part of your budget on the items that are on your extremities—your head, hands and feet.

■ Be an A-list lady by displaying beautiful behavior at all times.

## ABOUT THE AUTHOR

Dr. Stacia Pierce is a best-selling author, television personality, professional speaker, entrepreneur and life coach to thousands of people nationwide. For years, Dr. Stacia has focused solely on inspiring people and organizations from all walks of life and expanding their personal vision of what's possible.

A woman of candor and wit, she is widely known for her top-rated national television broadcast, *Successful Living with Dr. Stacia Pierce*, and for hosting the revolutionary International Women's Success Conference, which draws thousands of women each year to Lansing, Michigan. Several political dignitaries have recognized the conference as one of the most influential events for women.

In addition to her television broadcasts and outstanding events, Dr. Stacia can also be seen through a live webcast on The Word on Demand. Dr. Stacia has written more than twenty books, and has a vast library of resources and materials. Her training materials are widely used in churches, schools and corporate settings.

Dr. Stacia resides in Lansing, MI with her husband, Dr. James Pierce, and is also an outstanding mother to two children: daughter, Ariana and son, Ryan Pierce.

## Other Books by Dr. Stacia Pierce

25 Ways Women Can Motivate Themselves

25 Ways Ordinary Women Can Live Extraordinary Lives

25 Ways Moms Can Raise Extraordinary Kids

25 Habits of Successful Women

The Success Secrets of a Reader

Enjoy Life

Success Dress

The Making of a New You

Confession:  The Key to Purposeful Living

The Feminine Factor

The Power of Vision:  Framing Your Future with Your Imagination

Pursue Your Purpose and Live Your Dreams

Unlocking Your Creativity and God Ideas

# At Last! A Website to Empower Your Dreams and Make Success Your Reality!

*Dr. Stacia Pierce*

Lifestyle Coach to the Nation - Inspiring Women to Succeed - Redefining the Quality of Your Life

Visit www.ministry4women.com and explore the world of Dr. Stacia Pierce for the tools and inspiration to make success a cinch. This easy to navigate site, will provide you with product information, news, updates, downloads, advice and blogs all to make your life better!

# Log on Today!
# www.ministry4women.com

# Today's Dreams Determine Your Tomorrow!

Anyone who has achieved success started with a vision to achieve and become more. *The Prayer & Purpose Planner* is an easy to use system from Dr. Stacia Pierce which captures your vision and translates it into powerful pictures and words to help you see your way to success.

This is the roadmap to your dreams you've been waiting for. This incredible tool will help you to catalog and act on your dreams. You will be empowered to:
* Visualize better ideas and strategies for your success.
* Chart your progress and stay encouraged to succeed.
* Plan with pictures to accelerate the execution of your goals.

Go beyond your reality and envision new possibilities with Dr. Stacia's *Prayer & Purpose Planner.* Now is the time to do something about your dreams. If you've ever wanted to see beyond today and succeed in the future, *The Prayer & Purpose Planner* is for you. Invest now, get your Planner and begin framing your future. Before you know it, you'll flow with ideas that will help you to bring your Planner pages to life!